Market Speculating

The financial markets were once the preserve of City traders, but through the exciting and rapidly developing medium of spread betting, private investors can trade futures, options and other financial products.

Now, at last, it is easy for smaller investors to employ the same advanced profit-building strategies that have been used for years by professionals in the City. And under current legislation gains are tax free: all you have to pay is a small spread, the equivalent of a broker's commission.

This ground-breaking book, the first on the subject, details spread betting techniques, explores the principal markets and offers essential advice for all investors.

Foreword by Stuart Wheeler, Chairman of IG Index

Other books published by Rowton Press Ltd

Spread Betting by Andrew Burke

The Inside Track by Alan Potts
Against the Crowd by Alan Potts

Betting for a Living by Nick Mordin
Mordin on Time by Nick Mordin
The Winning Look by Nick Mordin

One Hundred Hints for Better Betting by Mark Coton

Coups and Cons by Graham Sharpe

For further details, credit card orders or information on forthcoming titles please call Rowton Press on:

01691 679111

or write to:

Rowton Press Ltd, PO Box 10, Oswestry, Salop SY11 1RB

also publishers of

ODDS*On* magazine

RP
ROWTON PRESS

MARKET SPECULATING
by **ANDREW**BURKE

RP
ROWTON PRESS

Market Speculating is sponsored by IG Index plc

Cover design by Pure Design & Advertising Ltd, Shrewsbury.

All rights reserved.
Unauthorised duplication contravenes applicable laws.
Any errors are our own for which we disclaim any responsibility.

© Rowton Press Ltd 1999

First Published 1999
by Rowton Press Ltd,
P.O.Box 10, Oswestry,
Shropshire SY11 1RB.

Typeset by Rowton Press using MICROSOFT WORD FOR WINDOWS
Output on a Hewlett Packard HP Laserjet 4000.

Printed and bound in Great Britain by MFP Design & Print, Manchester

1-871093-38-4

Foreword

This book tells you the best way to back your judgement on financial markets. The answer is spread betting. Why betting? For technical reasons it gives significant tax advantages, and you will be dealing, when you deal with IG Index, my company, with a Securities and Futures Authority regulated firm, just as you would with a stockbroker. Spread betting is the simplest form of betting. You may have been told that that is not so, but I am going to stick to my guns. Spread betting on financial markets really is simple, but there are two reasons why some people do not think so.

The first reason why people think spread betting is complicated is that we were all brought up to think that betting meant odds betting. That is what we learnt first and that is what we are used to and understand. Fair enough, but all I am saying is that you would feel the same way about spread betting, except more so, if you had started on that instead of on fixed odds. You would realise how simple spread betting is.

The second reason why people think financial spread betting is complicated brings me right to the point of this book. No one, and I mean no one, has, until now, written even reasonably well on the subject of financial spread betting. Most of what is written is turgid or unclear or both. That is why I had the idea of trying to persuade Andrew Burke to write this book. Andrew has indeed completely changed the situation. This book is highly readable, and very clear and accurate. As those of you who have read anything else he has written will agree, this comes as no surprise. To be a good writer you have to take a lot of trouble, but effort is not all – you have to have the talent.

6 . Market Speculating

Andrew does have the talent, and that is why you are going to enjoy the book. As you will have seen IG Index, which is the leader in financial spread betting, in its 25th year, is the sponsor of the book. So I would be complimentary about it, wouldn't I? Well, Yes, but the compliments are deserved.

You can treat financial spread betting as a hobby or as a business. If you want to treat it as a hobby you may perhaps want to use our Index Direct service, which offers very low minimum stakes and maximum simplicity. If you want to take it more seriously, and for serious money, that is fine too. IG will be happy to accommodate you for large stakes. Tax-free fortunes have been made through us. Of course you can lose large amounts too but IG provides a method by which you can put an absolute limit on your losses – so even when using large stakes you can sleep at night! In this book you will read, and easily understand, these and the many other advantages financial spread betting offers; the ability to back a price to go down – going short in the jargon – as well as up; how to use spread bets to hedge a share portfolio; the huge tax advantage – no capital gains tax to pay on your gains*; and very low minimum bet sizes. You may well be interested in the ability to take, through IG, a bull or bear position in any of 350 individual shares, on terms which not only contain all the advantages described above, but are cheaper than dealing through a stockbroker.

Andrew, however, also devotes a considerable part of the book to what many people find the most useful tool for predicting market movements – technical analysis. This too is explained with admirable clarity, and Andrew makes a most important point for those of us who may be sceptical about charts – that even if you do not have quite the same confidence in them that some do, you simply have to be aware of them. Because so many other people are watching them, prices will behave in ways that are influenced by charts, once certain points are reached. In other words to some extent the messages of charts are self-fulfilling prophecies.

There is another part of the book to which I especially commend your attention, the piece on money management. Shortly after leaving

---
* *Tax law can of course be changed.*

school I had a spectacular run of success on the horses. My bank was still the one I, and many other boys, had used at school. The bank manager, seeing bookmakers' cheques entering my account which were large for someone of my age, wrote me a charming letter. He had seen it all so many times before, he said, and in the end it was always the initial triumph which caused the ultimate disaster. I took no notice – of course! How I later wished that I had! So please take notice of Andrew's wise words.

Incidentally, we are a leader in sports spread betting too. Our takeover of the sports spread betting side of Ladbrokes in 1998 gave a big impetus to our already rapidly growing sports spread betting department.

Now let me hold you up no longer, because you want to read the book and I want you to become one of our customers!

Stuart Wheeler, Chairman IG Index plc

8 . Market Speculating
LIMIT THE RISK

If you are interested in spread betting, but don't want to risk a lot of money, the answer is

- Small minimum bet sizes.
- The maximum amount you can lose on any bet is strictly limited – your potential profit is not.
- Your profits are free from UK capital gains tax and income tax.* (We pay the betting duty.)
- You can deal with us directly over the internet. Take a look at our website:

www.indexdirect.co.uk

To find out more call Peter Martin:
FREEPHONE 0800-358-5599
Fax: 0171-896-0010
e-mail: info@indexdirect.co.uk

Index Direct is a division of IG Index plc., 1 Warwick Row, London SW1E 5ER

Risk warning: Spread bets carry a high level of risk to your capital. Only speculate with money you can afford to lose. Spread betting may not be suitable for all investors, so ensure that you fully understand the risks involved and seek independent advice if necessary.
*Tax law can, of course, be changed and may differ if you pay tax in a jurisdiction other than the UK.

Contents

Section One – Introduction

1. Why spread betting?   12
2. The basics   21

Section Two - Major markets

1. Betting on stock market indices   28
2. Betting on currencies   36
3. Betting on individual shares   42
4. Betting on interest rates   49
5. Betting on commodities   54

Section Three – Options   64

Section Four - Trading strategies

1. Managing risk   76
2. Getting through the early months   86

10 . **Market Speculating**

    3 Technical Analysis I: 93
       An introduction to charting

    4 Technical Analysis II: 108
       Beyond charts

    5 Money management   118

    6 How to cut dealing costs   126

    7 The ten golden rules   133

Section Five -
Investor protection and regulation   144

Appendices

    1 Further reading   152

    2 Recommended websites   156

Section One

Section One

Introduction

1 Why spread betting?

It may not attract a lot of headlines, and plenty of investors still seem to know little or nothing about it, yet spread betting has quietly emerged as one of the fastest growing sectors of the entire financial services industry.

Already more than 10,000 people have placed at least one financial spread bet, and the number of active traders is growing rapidly all the time. The financial bookmakers report that their turnover has grown by around 60 per cent per annum for each of the past two years. With further growth in sight, this is a business that can only get bigger and bigger.

It's not hard to understand why so many people, from so many backgrounds, with all kinds of varying objectives, are starting to develop an interest in spread betting.

As a group, private investors are becoming more sophisticated and better educated. Increasingly they want to take control of their own finances. They want to make decisions for themselves, and they want access to the same range of markets, derivatives and other products that in the past have only been available to the super-rich and to City professionals managing other people's money. For the first time, spread betting has made all this possible.

A world of opportunity is opening up for the smaller investor. 'Buy and hold' is no longer the only game in town. Spread bettors now have the freedom to speculate, to hedge, to sell short, to trade obscure commodities; in fact, to do just about anything the professionals do.

Selling short

For many investors one of the most exciting aspects of spread betting is that it provides a practical way of selling a market short; in other words betting that the market will fall.

Financial markets do not always rise in a straight line, as you've probably noticed, and almost all active investors want to have at least the option of betting that prices will head south.

Short selling can be used in many ways – as a near-term trading tactic to boost returns in a range-bound market; or for hedging; or to take a longer-term speculative view.

There are plenty of markets that in recent years have only been profitable for sellers. The Japanese stock market, for instance, is lower today than it was a decade ago, and the prices of many commodities have collapsed as the world's economy has slowed in the aftermath of

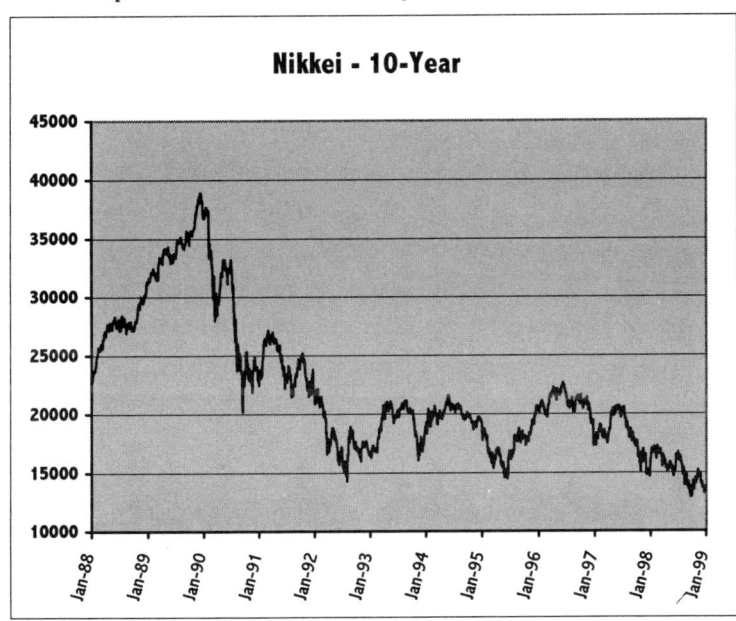

the Asian crisis. The oil price, for example, is lingering at 12-year lows, despite occasional fireworks in the Gulf.

The major Western stock markets, which most people tend to focus on, have all enjoyed spectacular, trend-busting gains in recent years. Selling short, occasional corrections aside, has proved to be a great way to lose money fast.

At the back of most people's minds, though, is an awareness that circumstances change. Markets move in cycles and even the optimists must admit that a bear phase is long overdue. Equity valuations are widely perceived to be stretched, particularly in America. Today, quality companies like Microsoft are priced on multiples of 25 – that's 25 times sales, not earnings. And a growing number of start-up enterprises, with names like Noprofitsyet.com, are commanding billion-dollar price tags.

Everyone's favourite bull may keep on charging. But after his recent exertions, he may just keel over and die. Smart investors will want to have the option of selling short, just in case.

Hedging

Most spread bets are exactly that – gambles. The investor takes a considered view of a particular market and backs the view with money. If he gets it right, the profits can be spectacular. If things don't work out ... well, the damage can be just as great.

There's nothing intrinsically wrong with this sort of high-risk/high-reward trading. Speculation has always been an integral part of the financial markets. People like George Soros and thousands of lesser-known fund managers are doing it every day with billions of pounds of their own and other people's money. Private investors should be free to join in, just so long as they understand the risks, act responsibly and trade with risk capital they can afford to lose.

However, not everyone wants to take risks. Some investors are quite anxious to avoid them (there's just no accounting for taste).

Selling short with a spread bet can be a very cost-effective way for cautious investors to limit risk.

For example, suppose you have a large exposure to the UK stock market, as many people do, either through directly owned shares, or indirectly via unit trusts and the like.

You may develop a view that the stock market is set for a fall in the short- or medium-term and that you want to protect yourself against this threat.

The obvious thing to do would be to sell the shares, bank the money and re-invest when the market had fallen or when things looked less ominous.

The catch is that getting in and out of equities is costly, often very costly. Brokers fees and stamp duty have to be paid. Dealing spreads have to be covered and, for people sitting on substantial paper profits, there can be considerable capital gains tax liabilities. Moving out and then back into the market can easily cost five to ten per cent of the value of a portfolio. So unless you expect a full-blown crash, selling shares is just not a cost-effective proposition.

This is where spread betting comes in. It's possible to sell the market short, either placing a down-bet on an index such as the FTSE-100, or even betting against individual shares (IG Index will offer a price on any company in the FTSE-350). If the market were to fall, any loss in the value on your shares would be covered by the profits from the spread bet, more or less.

Hedging in this way has its own costs, of course, but these are considerably lower than those associated with selling the underlying shares.

Those unfamiliar with spread betting can get a little concerned when you start talking about gambling on the financial markets but, as this sort of example shows, financial betting does not necessarily go hand in hand with increased risk. As we'll see later, all spread bets are only ever as risky as you allow them to be.

Leverage

In addition to making short selling possible, one of the other big attractions of spread betting is that it provides investors with a degree of gearing, or leverage. This means that relatively large amounts of money can be won with a fairly small outlay.

For instance, if you were to invest £2,000 directly on the stock market, depending on which shares you bought, you wouldn't expect to win or lose more than a few hundred pounds in a year. If you were to take that same money and use it for spread betting, again depending on which markets you chose to play, the returns could easily be a multiple of the original sum.

Thanks to spread betting, even with a relatively modest amount of risk capital it's possible to gain a meaningful exposure to the financial markets.

Naturally, leverage is not necessarily a good thing. It's very much a two-way street. With the wrong choice of bet, on a bad day, it is possible to lose far more than you ever expected, and some people do.

There are, however, ways in which you can gain most of the benefits of leverage whilst limiting the risks. You can employ what are known as controlled-risk bets, for example, or set stop-loss limits, or bet against certain kinds of options.

We'll look at all of these techniques more closely in subsequent chapters.

Diversification

Spreads also give smaller investors the chance to gain portfolio exposure at a relatively low cost.

Investment theorists have long argued that diversifying your investments is the best way to reduce risk and optimise total returns.

The dilemma for most investors is that it takes time and a significant amount of money to acquire an adequately diversified portfolio of shares.

An alternative is to place a spread bet on a broad market index such as the FTSE-100. It gives you instant, balanced exposure to the top 100 shares. Betting on the FTSE is the single most popular spread bet and the dealing costs are extremely competitive.

Range of markets

A further attraction of spread betting is that it offers access to every financial market you could ever wish to trade.

Most investors really don't have that much choice when it comes to deciding where to put their money. It's relatively easy to buy UK shares and gilts - and that's about it. It is possible to trade overseas markets directly but the dealing costs tend to be prohibitive.

Any investor seeking broad exposure to foreign markets is usually forced to go through managed funds, such as unit trusts.

The catch is, the fund management industry has a poor track record. Whatever those huge ads in the weekend personal finance supplements may say, the truth is that most fund managers are no better at picking winners than the fabled monkey tossing darts at a list of shares pinned to the wall.

Large funds are costly to run and it's hard for fund managers to outperform the market when, in effect, they are the market. This is why so-called tracker funds, which aim simply to mirror a particular stock market index, have mushroomed in recent years. Many investors would do just as well cutting out the middleman and handling their own affairs.

Spread betting offers investors access to just about every major financial market on the planet. All the world's major stock market indices are covered. It's possible to bet on interest rates, every currency of significance, and any commodity you care to name, from gold to pork bellies. In all, over 500 individual markets are priced up every day.

Which is not to say that you should rush to the phone straight away and start dabbling in cocoa futures.

Most investors, wisely, stick to the markets they know best. Betting on the FTSE typically accounts for about a third of all spread bets, and Wall Street contributes another 20 per cent. Turnover on commodities makes up only about two per cent of the total and such business as there is usually comes from market participants.

Whether you want to trade the Nikkei, sell the dollar, take a view on interest rates, or gamble on gold, spread betting makes it possible.

Why not trade direct?

Spread betting is not, of course, the only way to hedge, sell short, trade currencies or gain leverage. Futures and options offer exactly the same possibilities. Indeed, most spread bets are actually bets on futures and options. A punt on the FTSE, for example, is actually a bet on the direction of a FTSE futures contract, not a bet on the direction of the cash market itself.

Futures and options have one significant advantage over spread bets. Apart from bets on individual shares, where spread betting beats all the alternatives, futures and options are usually cheaper. If you were to bet on the FTSE via a futures contract, it would probably cost you two or three points less than an equivalent spread bet.

Despite this apparent price advantage, there are very good reasons why many investors prefer to go the spread betting route. The main reason has to do with taxation.

Anyone making a profit on a futures contract may become liable for capital gains tax. There is an annual exemption limit, currently £6800 a year, which covers gains from all sources, but for many investors this is not a tough limit to break.

Profits from spread bets, on the other hand, are not taxed, either as capital gains or as income. The reason for this, courtesy of a long-standing point of law, is that the returns from bets of any description are not taxable. The authorities recognise that if we had to hand over a share of our betting profits, we would also be entitled to offset any gambling losses, and as a brief visit to any betting shop will confirm, that would not be a healthy situation for the exchequer.

There is a small amount of betting duty to be paid. The bookmakers take account of this in the prices they quote, which is one of the reasons why spreads cost a little more than futures contracts.

For many, perhaps even most investors, tax is not a decisive issue. Most people do not bet in large enough volumes to threaten the CGT exemption limit. However, for a minority of bigger players the tax issue is absolutely critical – it's the one over-riding reason why they prefer spread betting to trading directly in the futures market.

Whether tax considerations are important to you will depend on your own financial circumstances. If there is even a possibility that any profits will be taxed then it would be foolish to trade any other way.

For those involved in the financial markets day-by-day (and around 30 per cent of spread punters work in the City in some capacity or other) tax is by no means the only advantage spreads hold over futures.

The futures market works differently: it's order driven. This means that when you want to trade, you have to contact your broker, place an order and wait for it to be executed. This takes time and there is no guarantee the order will be filled. Mostly this isn't a problem. But for a professional who perhaps knows that a big order is about to go through the market and who needs to deal without delay, it's quicker to call a spread bookmaker who will quote a firm price and take a bet instantly. Again, for most people, this is not a huge concern, but for some professionals it is important.

The other reasons why many professionals favour spreads is because certain markets are only offered by the spread firms, such as a daily FTSE bet, and also because they will often trade outside market hours. IG, for example, quote the major markets 24 hours a day.

For the smaller private investor these points are often academic. Tax is rarely a factor and a few seconds delay on a trade is hardly critical. There is, however, one huge reason why spread betting has the edge over futures and options, and it's all to do with access.

If you happen to have £50,000 of risk capital burning a hole in your bank account on Guernsey, you have to make a decision between spread betting and conventional derivatives. If you have £5,000 of risk capital, there really is no choice. It's spread betting or nothing.

Perhaps, in the future, private clients will be better catered for. But for now, the futures and options markets are simply not geared up to deal with ordinary investors.

The brokers don't offer credit in the way the spread firms do on many of their accounts. They insist on a - usually very large - cash deposit up-front.

The minimum bet sizes are much lower with the spread firms than in the derivatives markets. For example, the smallest spread bet on the FTSE, using IG's new Index Direct service is £2 a point. On a futures contract it's five times that. Anyone buying or selling a single FTSE futures contract would have to be prepared to win or lose anything up to £2,000 a day, and for most of us that's a little outside our comfort zone.

Sadly it seems that the major futures and options brokers simply have no interest in providing a service for ordinary investors. Smaller private clients are viewed as being too costly to handle. So unless you can slap down a five-figure cheque by way of a deposit, don't expect a warm welcome.

So the big attraction of spread betting for most people is the unique access it provides. It allows us to trade in reasonable amounts, when we want, on the markets we choose.

Thanks to spread betting even relatively small investors can at last use the same techniques and strategies as the professionals. If you're an active investor, you owe it to yourself to learn as much as possible about spread betting and to ensure that you have at your disposal as wide a range of options as possible.

Section One

Introduction

2 The basics

Approaching spread betting for the first time can be intimidating. The manner of trading is new to most people, and when you open an account the spread firms will provide you with so much detailed information, and such a comprehensive list of rules and regulations, that it's easy to feel swamped.

In essence, though, the basics of spread betting are incredibly simple. A few minutes spent working through some straightforward examples is all it takes to get to grips with the key points.

From a technical point of view, spread bets are what are known as contracts for differences. This means that you strike a bet at one level, close it at another, and the difference represents your profit or loss. Contracts of this kind are widely used in the financial markets and provide the basis for futures trading, among other things.

The easiest way to illustrate how a bet works is to take an example.

Let's consider a bet on the FTSE-100, the index that covers the top one hundred shares on the London stock exchange.

Let's say the index is currently trading at 6000 and you want to bet that it's heading higher.

There are always several FTSE contracts to choose from - we'll look at why in the next chapter – but let's suppose you reckon the market is going to move sooner rather than later, so you opt for the current

22 . Market Speculating

month and ring your bookmaker for quotes.

The dealer on the other end of the phone offers you a two-way price, let's say 6020-6030. This means that you can 'sell' and bet lower than 6020, or 'buy' and bet higher than 6030. The price quoted is slightly above the current level of the FTSE because it's a price for the future, and it's adjusted upwards to take account of interest rates and other considerations. Again, we'll look more closely at this in the next chapter.

The dealer quotes a 'spread' of two prices (hence spread betting) because, in the best traditions of trading, the firms make their money by charging different prices to buyers and sellers.

It's worth noting that when you phone for a price, the dealer has no way of knowing whether you want to buy or sell. And, of course, if you don't like the price, there is no obligation to bet.

In this example, as you expect the market to rise, you tell the dealer that you want to buy at 6030. You also have to nominate a unit stake, say £5 a point.

Let's be charitable and assume that everything goes according to plan. The index shoots up and a few days later the FTSE stands at 6200. You decide to bag the profit.

Once more you ring the dealer and ask for a price. The quote has now moved up to 6220-6230. As you have a 'long' position of £5, in order to close this out you have to sell £5, this time at the lower of the two prices quoted, 6220.

Your profit from the transaction would be as follows:

Closed at	6220
Opened at	6030
Difference	190
x Unit Stake	£5.00
Profit	£950.00

Not bad for a week's work. Of course, had you expected the market to fall and sold initially, rather than bought, the losses would have been on a similar scale. To be more precise, if, when the market was trading at 6000, you sold £5 at 6020, and then closed out by buying £5 at 6230, the consequences would have been as follows:

Closed at	6230
Opened at	6020
Difference	210
x Unit Stake	£5.00
Loss	£1050.00

The returns shown here are net returns. There are no fees or commissions of any kind to be paid. There is betting duty, but the bookmaker covers this out of his spread and, as mentioned in the previous chapter, there are no capital gains or income tax liabilities to worry about. The pricing is all highly transparent. Where spread betting is concerned, what you see is absolutely what you get.

You may notice that although these two sets of bets exactly mirror one another, there's a £100 discrepancy between what might have been won and lost. This is, of course, accounted for by the spread. On paper at least, though rarely in practice, the bookmaker makes a profit of half the spread x the unit stake every time a customer opens or closes a position. What's more, provided the buyers and sellers balance out, the bookmaker doesn't care which way the market goes – his profit is the same either way.

The size of the spread is very important. It varies according to which market is being traded, the unit stake, and it can even narrow or widen depending on the time of day. If you trade FTSE to small stakes outside of market hours, for instance, expect to pay more for the privilege.

Generally, the more liquid the market and the more business being done, the lower the spread. The exact details are set out in the bookmakers' dealing handbooks. As a rule, the wider the spread, the harder it is for the investor to make a profit. So you should always favour those markets with the lowest spreads. The FTSE certainly falls into this category.

Where all spread bets are concerned the returns, whether positive or

24 . Market Speculating

negative, vary according to how right or wrong you are. The more right you are, the more money you make; the more wrong you are, the more you lose.

This degree of proportionality makes spread betting a flexible and fair way to bet. Even if you get things slightly wrong - and everyone does from time to time - it's okay, because the losses should be reasonably modest.

Problems only really start to mount when you get a trade badly wrong, so it's very important to reduce the chances of this happening. Later on we'll consider what sort of steps you can take to reduce the risks.

Let's take another example now, this time from the currency markets.

Let's say the pound is trading at $1.6800 and you want to bet that it will strengthen relative to the dollar.

It's March now. You expect the move to happen gradually, so you get a quote for the June British pound/US dollar forward rate (the dealing months are all listed in the bookmakers' trading manuals). The spread quoted is 1.6740-1.6780. The slight difference between today's spot rate and the price in June is accounted for by the difference in interest rates between the US and Britain.

When trading currencies it's vital to understand which way round the quote is.

If you buy, you are betting that the first-named currency will strengthen.

If you sell, you are betting that the first-named currency will weaken.

In this case, because you want to bet that sterling will rise against the dollar, you need to buy at 1.6780. As the bet is in dollars, your stake will be denominated in dollars also. Let's say you bet $2 a point. A 'point' is the last figure in the quote, so in this example you win or lose $2 for every 0.0001 move in the exchange rate.

A month has passed, and the spot rate has moved up to $1.7000, as you had hoped, and you feel it's time to close out.

The spread has now moved to 1.6950-1.6990. Having bought to

open the position, you now have to sell to close, this time at 1.6950. The profit would be as follows:

Closed at	1.6950
Opened at	1.6780
Difference	0.0170

The profit, then, is 170 points multiplied by $2, or $340.

Any profit or loss is usually converted back into sterling when the bet is settled.

What if the bet had moved the other way? Again, let's assume the spread was bought for $2 at 1.6780, but that this time the spot rate fell from 1.6800 to 1.6600.

The quote for June would now be around 1.6550-1.6590 and the loss would be calculated as follows:

Opened at	1.6780
Closed at	1.6550
Difference	0.0230

The loss is 230 points multiplied by $2, or $460.

As with the FTSE bet, that 40-point spread ensures that you win slightly less when you get things right than you lose when you get them wrong.

And that, basically, is all there is to financial spread betting - you open a bet at one level, close it at another, and multiply the result by your stake. The details of the markets traded may vary, but the underlying process never changes.

If this is all new to you, it's worth going back over these examples a few times and making sure you understand them. It's also worth spending some time reading through the manuals the spread firms produce and studying the examples contained in them.

The next step is try a few phantom trades of your own, 'opening' and 'closing' fictional positions but using realistic, if imaginary stakes, and real-time prices. You can get the prices off the Internet, off Teletext, or ring up for them.

26 . Market Speculating

This should all become second nature very quickly, but if you have any questions, always contact the spread firms. New accounts are being opened constantly and the dealers are used to explaining things to new clients. Certainly it's vital to be absolutely clear about what you're doing, and what the risks are, before you put money on the line and open your first real position.

Section Two

Section Two

Major markets

1 Betting on stock market indices

Although spread betting offers investors the chance to take a view on practically any financial market anywhere in the world, the vast bulk of business is concentrated into just a handful of areas.

Inevitably the big equity markets tend to dominate. Greatest interest, as we have seen, is in the FTSE-100, and betting on it accounts for about a third of all turnover. Perhaps surprisingly, the American markets lag not far behind. Anything up to a quarter of all bets are placed on the key US indices.

The other two dozen or so equity indices that are priced up every day tend to appeal to professionals and to a few dedicated specialists. The big Far Eastern markets, like Japan's Nikkei 225 and Hong Kong's Hang Seng index, are closely watched, but they trade overnight and are hard for private investors to keep track of.

These Asian markets have been perceived in the past as somewhat risky to trade, and they certainly are volatile. But with IG setting new minimum bets as low as 50p a point, the stakes are now such that smaller investors may feel encouraged to start taking positions.

The better known continental indices, such as France's CAC 40 and Germany's Dax, have never really fired the imagination of most speculators.

The leading stock market indices dominate spread betting for a variety of reasons.

To begin with, these markets will always be used for hedging. This may only represent a small part of overall betting activity, but it does guarantee a certain minimum level of turnover.

More to the point, quoted companies and the indices they make up are familiar to all of us. Information on equities is widely available and is discussed in detail both in the financial press and in the mainstream media. Most active investors know far more about the stock market than they do about any other part of the financial universe. And not unlike property prices, we all have a view on valuations. It's no surprise that most spread punters start here.

What's more, betting on the leading market indices is actually quite a smart thing to do. It's far easier to stay on top of developments when trading the FTSE than when trading, say, commodities or bonds issued by foreign governments. Plus, and this is a critical point, the spreads on the main indices tend to be lower than on any other markets. For the smaller investor this is absolutely the most sensible area upon which to focus attention.

Most, though not all, index bets are bets on futures. Futures and spread bets are quite similar, both are contracts for differences and both offer a degree of leverage. The history of futures trading, though, rather pre-dates spread betting.

The futures market sprang into life more than a century ago, where else but in America.

At that time, the US Mid-West was opening up and becoming a vital source of food for the rest of America and for Europe. Crop and livestock prices, though, were unpredictable. Farmers were planting crops not knowing for sure whether they would be able to sell them for a profit the following year. And European importers faced their own difficulties, having to contend with volatile prices and unreliable sources of supply.

This uncertainty was hindering progress and a solution was sought. Ingeniously, a trading centre was set up in Chicago, at the heart of the Mid-West, where crops and livestock could be bought and sold, but

30 . Market Speculating

with delivery deferred until some pre-set point in the future. Now farmers could sell a crop long before it was harvested, making sure of a profit. And importers could plan ahead and buy up crops and livestock months before they needed them, guaranteeing a steady source of supply.

For a market like this to work, certain uniform standards had to be agreed. So contracts were always for the same specified quantity and quality of product. In reality, of course, when delivered, the crops or livestock would vary slightly from the terms of the contract, so the price would have to be adjusted to reflect this.

In order to make the new market as liquid as possible, it was decided to permit dealing on margin. In other words, anyone buying a contract had only to put up a fraction of the contract's value, at least initially. So, for example, someone buying a $1,000 cattle contract might only have to pay $100 up-front. If the value of the contract were then to rise by, say, 20 per cent to $1200, the purchaser could sell the contract on to someone else, pocketing a $200 profit in the process. A $200 profit on an actual investment of $100 is a return of 200 per cent.

The availability of trading on margin drew in speculators - people with absolutely no interest in buying or selling the underlying commodities, but who were trying to make money playing the market. The presence of speculators strengthened the market because, as intended, it boosted liquidity.

From a technical viewpoint, the new market was a means of redistributing risk, taking it away from the farmers and the importers and the other end users, and shifting it on to the speculators. In return for shouldering this risk, the speculators as a group, though not necessarily as individuals, could expect to make a small profit at the expense of the end-users.

The producers and wholesalers, for their part, were happy to sacrifice a small premium in return for the stability that the new market brought to their businesses.

That's the origin of the futures markets. Just to be clear, a futures market is any place where standard commodities can bought and sold on margin for future delivery.

Not a lot has changed since those early days in Chicago. Corn and pork bellies are still traded in the Windy City, and the spread firms will make you a price if you want.

The one big innovation since then is that futures trading is no longer confined to physical commodities. In 1975, Chicago introduced the first financial futures, and in 1982 the London International Financial Futures Exchange, LIFFE, opened its doors. It's on this exchange that FTSE futures are traded.

Most index spread bets are not on a stock market index itself, but on the futures contract. The spread firms prefer to bet on futures contracts for several reasons. Firstly, it's convenient – it provides a standard ready-made market that's the same for everyone across the industry. Secondly, the bookmakers can price a market faster and with greater confidence if they can take quotes directly from an exchange. Thirdly, and perhaps most importantly, it provides the spread firms with a means of hedging. They can trade the futures contract for their own account if their liabilities move outside acceptable limits. Indeed, a great many spread bets actually end up aggregated and hedged directly in the futures market.

The spread firms outline which contracts they bet on in their dealing handbooks and you need to read the relevant information before trading. You should note that the range of contracts offered is not the same for all firms

It's very important to understand that betting on a futures contract is not the same as betting on the underlying market, though the two are obviously linked.

The FTSE-100 index, for example, has a hundred separate components and will move up or down more slowly than the futures contract, which is a single market that can factor in developments more quickly.

Also, when Chicago let in the speculators a century ago, little did the founding fathers realise the extent to which the tail would one day wag the dog. Speculative money, and all the excesses that go with it, drive futures markets. So prices can be much more volatile than those in the underlying market. This is particularly true on the day a contract

32 . Market Speculating

expires, when, for technical reasons, the swings can be extreme.

A futures contract, and a spread bet on it, will often stand at a premium to the cash market, and the longer the life of the contract, the greater the premium is likely to be.

The premium is a function of interest rates and dividend expectations.

The yield on shares is lower than the interest paid on bank deposits. So an investor would, if the futures price were the same as the cash price, get a higher return by buying futures on margin, and then banking the rest of his cash, than he would if he simply used all of his money to buy shares. The premium cancels out this effect. It also takes account of the fact that someone trading futures receives no dividends.

What the premium is *not* is some kind of market prediction that share prices will rise. It's simply a mechanical adjustment to today's share prices.

Having said that, the futures market is a market like any other, driven by supply and demand, and a contract will often trade at a premium several points above or below the fair-value level.

A few index bets are not based directly on any futures contract, the daily FTSE and Wall Street markets being cases in point. IG also offers a Millennium FTSE, which is a bet on where the FTSE will close on the last trading day of 1999 – the LIFFE contracts don't go that far ahead.

The precise terms of dealing for index markets vary, but they have become a lot more demanding in recent years. Deposit requirements have risen sharply, reflecting the fact that markets are at much higher levels now than they used to be, and also that volatility is more of an issue. It was once possible to trade Wall Street for £10 a point with the spread firms if you had a £1,000 limit on your account. Now you need almost four times as much.

IG have got round this problem by setting up Index Direct, a new service for lower-staking clients – a category into which, frankly, most of us fall. As well as addressing risk issues, which we'll look at later, the new service offers much lower minimum bet sizes. It's now possible to trade FTSE or Wall Street for £2 a point. Over time, that can still mean thousands of pounds won or lost, but the consequences of a big daily move have become less dramatic.

Even at these more manageable levels, it's still important to know what you're doing. This includes understanding the characteristics of any indices you may wish to trade.

It's often assumed that the best-known indices are a fair reflection of the wider stock market, but this is not necessarily the case.

The main Wall Street index is particularly unrepresentative. It includes just 30 stocks, all huge, mature businesses like IBM, Coca-Cola, American Express and Boeing. The index is not even weighted by market capitalisation. (A company's market capitalisation, or market cap, is its share price multiplied by the number of issued shares, in other words it's the company's stock market value.)

Charles Dow, founder of the *Wall Street Journal*, conceived the index in 1896 and its popularity has more to do with its long history and with convention than with its reliability as a market proxy. Incidentally, Mr Dow's index is still copyright, which is why neither we nor the spread firms refer to it by name.

The S&P 500 is a far more accurate measure. It incorporates the top 500 quoted companies and weights them according to market cap. The S&P covers about 75 per cent of the value of the New York market.

The less well known Nasdaq Composite is also worth a look, particularly right now.

Many observers feel the US market is currently in the midst of a financial bubble, with the worst excesses centred on the high-tech sector. These things are notoriously hard to judge at the time, but when you see companies like the on-line bookseller Amazon.com, with no profits and just 600-odd employees, valued at $12 billion, you have to wonder. That sort of valuation, incidentally, would put Amazon comfortably in the top half of the FTSE if it were a UK company.

More than any other index, the Nasdaq is dominated by the high-tech sector, with industry Goliath's like Intel, Microsoft, Dell and Oracle figuring prominently.

Most spread bettors almost instinctively prefer to sell the traditional Wall Street 30-share index, and the spread firms report that there's

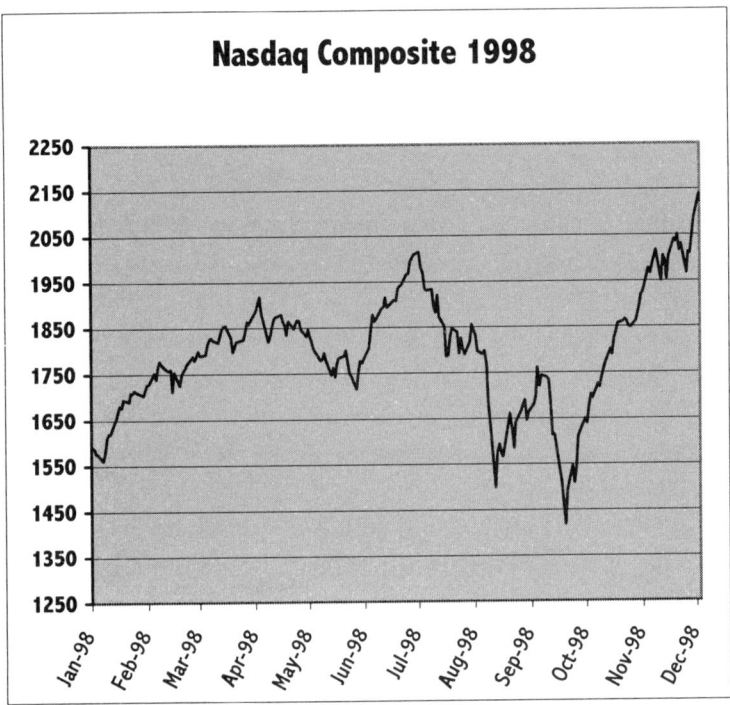

been heavy net selling of that index for years now. But if you really believe America is in the throes of a stock market mania, selling the Nasdaq might be a smarter proposition. High-tech shares have risen further than the major industrials and would have further to fall back in a crash. Besides, the Street's big blue chips might be regarded as a safe haven in a time of crisis.

Of course, this pre-supposes that US shares are over-valued, and that's not been a profitable view to hold in recent years. Far from it.

The FTSE is a reasonably representative measure of the London market, but it's not perfect. Certain sectors are over-represented, notably pharmaceuticals and financials.

There are three giant pharmaceutical companies – Glaxo, SmithKline Beecham and Zeneca - among the top dozen stocks in the FTSE. As the index is weighted by market cap, these three alone can distort the market. They have a greater impact, for example, than the bottom 30 shares combined. Anyone trading the FTSE has to be conscious of developments in the sector. A bid rumour, annual results, news of drugs trials, and so on, can all have a disproportionate impact on the index.

In addition to betting on futures, it's also possible to use index options to trade the market. But this is a specialist area, and we'll take a closer look at it when we cover options later in the book.

Section Two

Major markets

2 Betting on currencies

The foreign exchange market is, in many respects, the most important of all financial markets. It's certainly the biggest, and the volume of business carried out, even on the quietest of days, is stunning. It's also the one truly global financial market, with trading rolling seamlessly from Tokyo to London to New York as the business day evolves.

The basic function of the foreign exchange market (also known as the Forex, or FX market, depending on how abbreviated you want to get) is to provide a service for people and businesses who need to swap currencies. Exporters, for example, have to convert foreign earnings into domestic currency; tourists need their pesetas; and investment managers buy and sell currencies as they move assets round the globe.

This commercial trade, though, is just the tip of the iceberg. More than $1 trillion a day passes through the market, and though exact figures are hard to come by, it's estimated that international trade and mainstream investment transfers account for only around ten per cent of this. The balance, all 90 per cent of it, is purely speculative - investment banks, brokers, hedge funds and others, all gambling billions of dollars a day on fluctuations in exchange rates.

Eventually, currency rates are determined by fundamental economic forces. In the short-term, though, and sometimes even over the medium-term, interest rates and other factors matter a great deal less than the direction of these huge speculative flows of money. The amounts involved are so vast that not even governments can stem the flood, a lesson well learnt when sterling crashed out of the Exchange Rate Mechanism in 1992. The Bank of England threw billions of pounds at the market in a massive - and completely futile - attempt to see off the speculators. The end result was a devalued pound and a massive transfer of wealth from British taxpayers to mostly foreign speculators. The funds managed by George Soros famously notched up gains of £600 million in a matter of days, underscoring the almost incomprehensible scale of the FX market.

For the private investor, it's not easy making money on the currency market. This is a very liquid, efficient marketplace. When you trade, you are effectively locking horns with some of the largest, most sophisticated institutions in the world, and most of the advantages lie with them.

Unlike smaller investors, the big hedge funds, for example, pay virtually no spread at all when they trade – the banks they deal with want the business just so they know where that flood of speculative money is going. And the banks themselves also have access to a great deal of what might be called 'market intelligence'. They know, for instance, the levels at which their customers are placing buy and sell orders, so they have a pretty good idea of supply and demand in the market at particular price levels.

Though the hedge funds sometimes take longer-term views, most currency speculation is extremely short-term in nature. The standard approach is to deal in vast sums and make tiny percentage profits very quickly. If you ever happen to overhear a couple of traders discussing their work, you'll notice lots of casual references to 'yards' of this and 'yards' of that - a 'yard' being market slang for a billion dollars' worth of a currency. The FX market is no place for people bad with telephone numbers.

Fortunately, there are some respects in which the private investor has at least some sort of an edge.

Private investors have the freedom to develop much longer-term

38 . Market Speculating

views and, unlike market professionals who have to justify those big bonuses, we can sit tight for weeks, or even months, waiting for the right opportunity to come along.

It's certainly been possible for smaller investors to trade profitably in recent years. Dollar/yen, for instance, is one of the most closely followed of all the major rates. It's been very volatile throughout the past few years, and anyone spotting the trend early enough has been in a position to notch up substantial gains:

Charts play a big role in currency trading. The banks, brokers and hedge funds are all working with such short time horizons, trying to make money almost minute by minute, that underlying economic trends tend to play second fiddle to retracements, supports, break-outs and the other signs buried in the entrails of yesterday's price action. How much use charts are as a trading tool is open to debate, but the bottom line is that they are hugely influential in the currency markets, and before trading any currency you should know where the key technical levels are. The spread firms will be quite happy to fax you any chart you want.

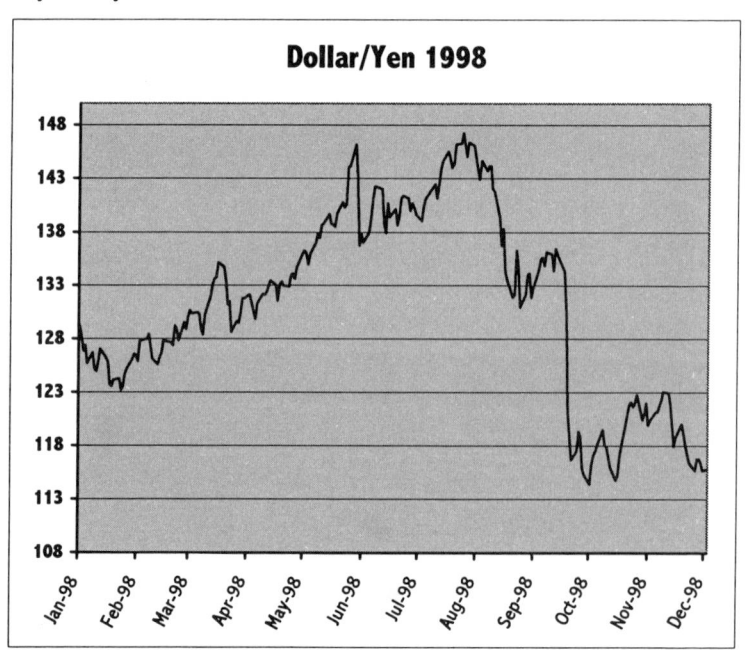

Dollar/Yen 1998

Spread betting on currencies comes in two varieties. As with equities, most bets are on futures (or forwards, which are pretty much the same thing). This allows investors to bet on what an exchange rate will be at some fixed point in the future. A range of contract months is offered, and these are set out in the dealing handbook.

The second kind of bet is a bet on the spot rate. It's a bet on today's exchange rate and is intended for very short-term trading.

The spread on the spot rate is much lower than the equivalent spread on a futures bet. For example, the standard spread on pound/dollar with IG is 24 points at the spot rate, 40 points at the forward rate.

If you expect a big move within a day, perhaps because some key technical level has been reached, or because some important data is due out, then the spot rate is the better option.

The catch is, though, that any move really does have to be big. Beating a 40-point spread over, let's say, a month is feasible. Beating 24 points in a matter of hours is, well, challenging.

Any bet at the spot rate that is not closed out the day it's opened is automatically rolled over to the following day. This means, technically, that the original bet is closed and a new, identical position opened for the following day. The catch is that the bookmaker charges for this, so continually rolling over can be costly.

If you plan to run a position for more than a few days, forget the spot rate and use a forward bet. The spread is higher, but it's still cheaper than rolling over.

The spot rate is simple to deal with because there are no premiums or discounts to confuse the issue. Quotes on forward rates, though, are always adjusted to reflect interest rates.

Interest rates have a huge impact on currencies. It's not hard to appreciate why. Other things being equal, would you rather deposit your money in Japan and earn zero per cent interest, or in Mexico and make 30 per cent? Unfortunately other things are not equal, so don't book that flight to Acapulco just yet. Forward exchange rates compensate for differences in interest rates. As with all futures markets, the calculation is a mechanical one and not some sort of crystal ball gazing exercise on the part of the market.

Pound/Dollar 1998

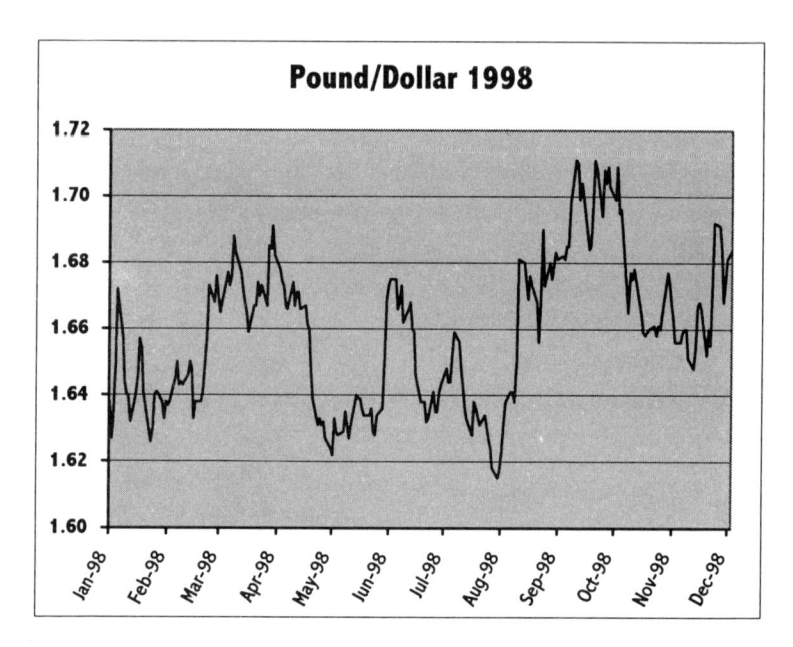

Usually, the more liquid and more commonly traded the market, the narrower the spread. In effect, it costs less to trade the major currencies, so for most people it makes sense to stick to dollars, yen, pounds and euros.

Many of those who trade currencies have at least some professional experience of the market. Investors who don't should make sure they know exactly what they're doing before committing hard cash. There are two points in particular to watch. Firstly – and forgive me if this sounds elementary – you have to be sure you have the bet you think you have.

Currency prices are not absolutes. Each exchange rate has two sides to it. This can cause confusion and it's important to understand which way round you're dealing. When you buy, you are betting that the first-named currency will strengthen. When you sell, you are betting that the first-named currency will weaken. So if you buy dollar/yen, you expect the dollar to strengthen against the yen. If you sell dollar/yen, you expect the dollar to fall against the yen. When you place a currency bet, the dealer will often take the precaution of spelling out what your position is. Or maybe that's just for my benefit.

The second point to watch is staking. Everyone has an intuitive feel for what a fiver bet on the FTSE represents. Most of us are less clear when trading currencies. Which bet is bigger, $10 a point of sterling/dollar, or $10 of euro/dollar?

The minimum stakes set out in the dealing handbook serve as a guide. A more sophisticated technique is to multiply the stake by the price in points. This gives the rough value of an equivalent transaction on the foreign exchange market.

Assuming sterling/dollar is trading at 1.6650 (or 16650 points), a $10 bet is the same as buying or selling $166,500 on the FX market. .

If euro/dollar is trading at 1.1650 (or 11650 points), a $10 bet is the same as buying or selling $116,500 on the FX market.

So clearly a $10 a point bet on sterling/dollar represents a bigger underlying position than the same size trade on euro/dollar.

Incidentally, isn't it amazing how an apparently small spread bet, like $10 a point, can actually be equivalent to a six-figure position in the foreign exchange market? If the exchange rate moves by ten per cent, you win or lose about $10,000.

A swing that wild would be unlikely in the case of sterling/dollar (or 'cable' as it's known in the trade). The two currencies tend to move more or less in tandem.

But dramatic moves greater even than ten per cent have been witnessed elsewhere recently, notably in dollar/yen. When these huge swings occur, events can evolve very quickly, and fortunes are often won and lost in the process.

Perhaps the best way for private investors to bet on currencies is to forget trying to predict daily fluctuations – leave that to the professionals. A better approach is to try to spot a developing trend and to stick with it for the medium-term.

As I write, a lot of experts feel the dollar will gradually weaken as central banks load up on the new euro. It may or may not happen, but this is the sort of broad trend you should be watching for. If you can latch on to such a move and run with it, serious profits can be made – even when the stakes are small.

Section Two

Major markets

3 Betting on individual shares

The most important development in financial spread betting recently has been the introduction of betting on individual shares.

In the past, the spread firms made a name for themselves during high profile flotations, creating a so-called 'grey market' and betting on where a company's share price would close at the end of the first day's trading. It was a risky business and something of an attention-grabber, particularly when some of the big state enterprises were being privatised.

Given that experience, it's surprising perhaps that the spread firms haven't moved sooner to meet the obvious demand that exists for betting in this area.

At the moment IG is the only firm offering prices on individual companies, but spread betting is nothing if not competitive and their rivals will almost certainly respond before long with similar services of their own.

Not so long ago it was only possible to trade a small number of leading companies, but the range of opportunities has broadened considerably over the past 12 months. Today it's possible to take a view on any company listed in the FTSE-100 or the FTSE Mid-250.

Extending the choice to the top 350 stocks listed in London has made this one of the most exciting areas for spread punters. For the non-professional, it's tough to form a view about Japanese government bonds; it's rather easier to have an opinion on what the future holds for Dixons, Next, Pizza Express, British Biotech or Manchester United.

In order to price so many stocks, IG have automated the process. Dealers work from a spreadsheet package that takes the current share price of any company, increases it to reflect interest rates, decreases it to allow for dividends foregone, and the end result is in effect a futures price for each company.

This area of betting highlights the advantages of spread betting very clearly. To begin with, it's possible to go short. This used to be fairly easy to do when the Stock Exchange ran an account trading system, but since its abolition, there is no other way for ordinary investors to profit from a negative view about a company. In the City, the institutions can and often do enter into contracts for differences with one another, and that's how IG hedges its exposure. But this option is out of bounds for small investors. If you want to sell short, spread betting is the only way to do it

The other big advantage this form of spread betting offers is

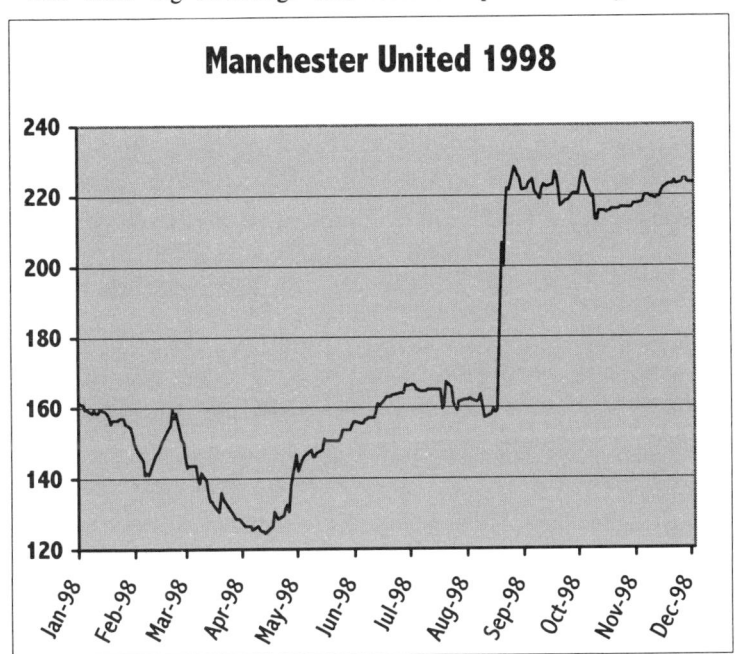

Manchester United 1998

44 . Market Speculating

leverage – the ability to assume a large position despite a relatively limited capital base. In fact, in some cases this can be done on credit, not tying up any capital at all.

Let's say, for example, that you're a fan of Dixons. You feel the company is well placed to profit from the explosion of interest in the Internet; you've checked the financial figures and like what you see; and you feel the share price might get a near-term technical boost if the company is added to the FTSE-100.

You could, of course, simply buy the shares. And for many investors – such as those who are risk-averse, have a diversified portfolio and who are prepared to take a three- to five-year view – this could well be the smart thing to do.

Let's suppose you have £5,000 of available capital and you use all of this to buy shares. Within a month the share price rises, say, ten per cent in value and you opt to cash in. After dealing expenses - the market spread, commissions and so on - the profit on the completed transaction would be perhaps a little over £300.

Now let's consider the alternative. Instead of buying shares, you open a spread bet. The current market price for Dixon's is 600p. The quote for a bet expiring in three months is 635-645. You buy £25 at 645.

Again, the underlying share price rises ten per cent, from 600p to 660p. The spread price will now be about 685-695. Once more, you decide to close out the position. The profit would be as follows:

Closed at	685
Opened at	645
Difference	40
x Unit Stake	£25.00
Profit	£1,000.00

Clearly, if your view of the market is correct, you can make far more money spread betting than trading actual shares. That's the power that leverage, or gearing, can offer an investor.

As always, though, the impact works both ways. Had the share price of Dixon's fallen, the losses would have been greater on the spread bet than they would have been from simply buying shares.

In addition to the double-edged benefits of gearing, and the flexibility of being able to sell short, spread betting on shares also has a certain price advantage over the direct buying and selling of shares. The combined effect of commissions, stamp duty and market spreads usually means that for the short-term investor it's simply cheaper to open a spread bet than to actually buy and sell shares.

For heavy-hitters this is even more true, because spread bets don't have the capital gains tax complications of direct share ownership.

Traditionalists, particularly those who work for stockbrokers, might not approve of betting on shares. The right way to play the stock market, they would argue, is to buy shares, not bet on them, and to hold those shares for at least three, and preferably five years or more.

That's sensible advice and few commentators would dispute that 'buy and hold' has been the best investment strategy for decades. The reality is, though, that many people just don't invest this way. And if you are going to trade the market actively, either with some of your capital or all of it, then it's simply more cost-effective to work through a spread firm than through a stockbroker.

Of course, betting on shares does not have to be risky, far from it. Bets on specific shares can be used to hedge existing investments.

In recent years, occasional spasms aside, the stock market has been a safe place to invest. The world's major stock markets have seen off an economic meltdown in Asia; a debt default in Russia; the near-collapse of the financial system as a multi-billion dollar hedge fund went bust in all but name; and the historic impeachment of a US president. All this, and the major indices just keep reaching for the sky. The need to hedge has not figured prominently on many agendas.

That may change in 1999. Sober voices are starting to question equity valuations in general, and the pricing of US tech stocks in particular. Maybe London and New York will have another year of double-digit gains, but just a little caution would not be out of place.

The standard way to lock-in market gains is to sell shares. But for many investors there are compelling reasons not to do so. The dealing costs can be substantial, particularly if the plan is to re-invest the money in the market at some point in the future when valuations are perhaps less demanding. And for larger investors, the capital gains tax implications can be considerable.

Spread betting offers a practical way of hedging that gets around these problems.

As we have noted earlier, one option is to continue holding the shares but to open a compensating short position with a spread bet. The dealing costs are lower than selling the shares, and there's no CGT liability. If the value of your shares falls, profits from the spread bet will cover the losses.

The other option is to sell the shares and bank the money, then to open a similar long position through a spread bet. This way, as well as earning interest on the capital, the spread bet provides exposure to the market should the share price of your favourite company continue to rise.

And, of course, you can hedge varying amounts of your equity holdings depending on how cautious your view is.

Most investors do not hedge. Let's face it, in recent years there's been no point. If we ever do experience a genuine bear market, though, like the one that Japanese investors have lived through for the past decade, perhaps attitudes to hedging will change.

For the time being, most spread punters bet on shares for no other reason than to try to turn a profit.

Most financial markets are tough places for smaller investors to make money.

Play the currency markets, for instance, and you might take on the collective muscle of every major financial institution in the world. You could still win, just as the banks and hedge funds themselves sometimes lose, but the odds are against you.

The stock market provides a much more favourable environment for small investors. The institutions still have some advantages, such as lower dealing costs and greater access to management, but the scales are less unbalanced than in any other area.

Investors in pursuit of value can choose from several approaches.

Section Two: Major markets . 47

Many investors react to market news. A company on the receiving end of takeover speculation will almost always attract buyers. Sometimes investors will try to take a view ahead of corporate results, anticipating good or bad figures. Sometimes a good story will provoke interest. Boardroom changes, a new product launch, a shift in strategic direction, or an upgrade or downgrade by a broker can all offer encouragement to speculators.

There's also the City's usual background noise of rumour and gossip, some of it reliable, some of it half-reliable, and much of it utter nonsense.

Perhaps naively, I asked the staff at IG whether betting on shares didn't leave them at the mercy of investors armed with inside information.

"Sometimes we do get caught out," replied a senior figure, "but most of the time clients trading on information generally know less than they think they do."

I guess that's a clever way of saying that markets are broadly efficient and that share prices tend to be quite accurate. So if you do decide to trade on information, make sure it's good information, not old news already discounted in the price.

Rather than reacting to stories, perhaps a more sensible approach is to go back to basics and study the businesses themselves. Aside from all the financial data publicly available, we all know an incredible amount about corporate UK.

Of the top 350 companies listed in London, most are household names. We know these firms and we know their products and services. We often work for these companies or do business with them, or our family or friends do. Whereas people who bet on rumours and gossip often know less than they think they do, the rest of us know far more about listed companies than we realise.

Of course, 99 per cent of the time what you know about Natwest or Asda or British Airways has no real investment value, but you only need to be right once to make money.

There was a wonderful example late in 1998. At the beginning of November, Marks & Spencer announced its first fall in profits for 30 years. The chairman, Sir Richard Greenbury, used words like "bloodbath", as he revealed that the company would not meet its sales targets for the year. Sales of non-food items – clothes, basically – were hardest hit. The share price fell ten per cent in response.

Now, M&S is not a small company. It employs 48,000 people. How many of those must have known sales were not on target? How many suppliers must have had an idea? How many other retailers must have recognised how tough trading conditions were on the high street? And that's to say nothing of the millions who shop at M&S, at least some of whom must have had their doubts about the product range. All of these people, to some degree or other, were in a position to know that M&S was in trouble long before the suits in the City ever realised there was a problem. And they could have backed the view and profited from it.

Okay, it's easy to spot the warning signs after the event, but there really are opportunities like this out there all the time. Do your homework, trade sensibly, and you really can make money betting on shares.

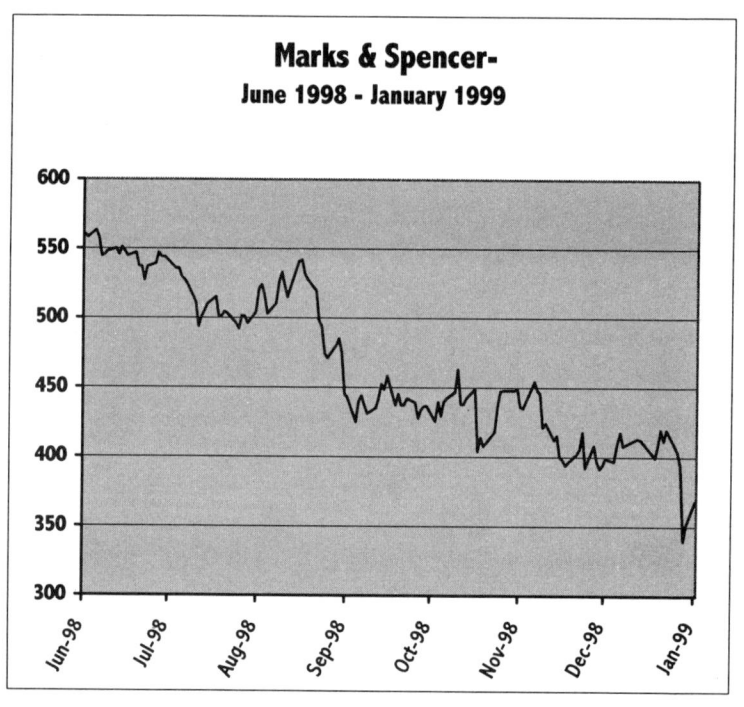

**Marks & Spencer-
June 1998 - January 1999**

Section Two

Major markets

4 Betting on interest rates

The level of interest rates in a country can be influenced by a range of factors including the state of the public finances, the strength of the economy and expectations about what's going to happen to inflation. If you have an opinion in one of these areas and you want to back it, then an interest rate bet offers the most direct way of doing so.

There are two broad categories of spread bets available on interest rates. Firstly there are contracts that allow you to bet on short-term, three-month interest rates in any one of several countries. Secondly there are government bond futures that reflect longer-term interest rates.

The key point to remember about the pricing of all interest rate bets is that there's an inverse relationship between price and the level of interest rates. In other words, when rates rise, the price of the contract falls; when rates fall, the price of the contract rises. So you have to buy when you expect rates to fall, and sell when you expect them to rise.

The easiest way to understand why this inverse relationship exists is to look at an example:

Suppose interest rates are currently at ten per cent. A bond with a face value of £100 is issued with an annual coupon, or dividend, of £10. Now, if interest rates rise to say 12 per cent, the value of the bond has to fall to £83.33 so that the £10 dividend represents a yield of 12 per cent.

50 . Market Speculating

The process also works in reverse. Taking the same £100 bond with a £10 dividend, if rates fall from ten per cent to eight per cent, the market value of the bond has to rise to £125 so that the £10 dividend equates to an eight per cent yield.

In real life, pricing interest rate products is a little more complex than this, but the basic relationship between rates and price holds true.

The most popular bet on short-term interest rates is the three-month Sterling Deposits contract traded on LIFFE, better known as 'short sterling'.

If you've never traded short sterling before, the way it's quoted can seem a little awkward at first. The value of a contract is 100 minus the implied interest rate. So if the June contract is trading at 94.50, the market expects that, in June, three-month interest rates will be at 5.50 per cent.

The contract is expressed in this way in order to maintain the traditional inverse relationship between price and interest rates; short sterling falls when rates rise, and rises when rates fall.

Let's take an example. Suppose June short sterling is trading at 94.50.

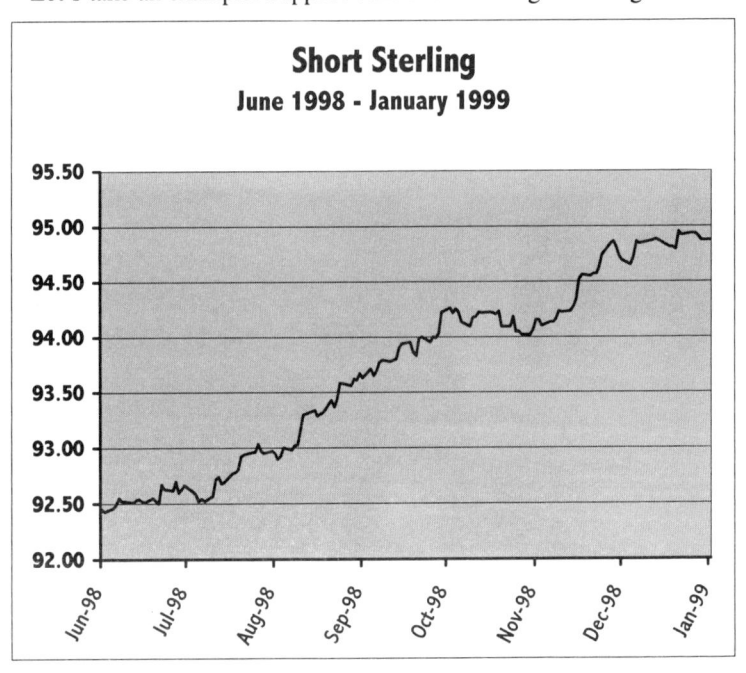

Short Sterling
June 1998 - January 1999

You expect interest rates to rise. The spread, from which the firms drop the decimal point, is 9447-9453. You sell £20 a point at 9447.

Over the next few weeks official data is released hinting at an economy starting to heat up, rates rise and the market moves in your favour. Short sterling is now 94.25. The spread firm quotes 9422-9428 and you opt to close. The profit would be as follows:

Opened at	9447
Closed at	9428
Difference	19
x Unit Stake	£20.00
Profit	£380.00

The bond markets, which are perhaps more familiar to many investors than the three-month markets, offer a way to bet on longer-term rates. It's possible to takes a view on UK gilts, US treasuries, Japanese government bonds and other selected bond markets.

Pricing works in the same inverse fashion as for short sterling, though US bond are rather quaintly quoted in fractions ($1/32^{nds}$), and this can cause confusion for those of us who went decimal back in the seventies.

To take an example: March treasury bonds are trading at 127–23, that's 127 and $23/32_{nds}$. You feel rates will rise and bond prices fall. The spread is 127–20 to 127–26, and you sell $15 at 127-20. That's $15 per $1/32_{nd}$

The market moves against you. Rates fall, bond prices rise, and the spread moves up to 128–2/128–8. You buy at 128-8 to close. The loss is as follows:

	Opened at	129-20
	Closed at	128-8
* ie $20/32_{nds}$	Difference*	20
	x Unit Stake	$15
	Loss	$300

As with all spread bets denominated in a foreign currency, this $300 would usually be converted back to sterling when the bet is settled.

Hopefully these examples demonstrate that although betting on interest rates is basically quite straightforward, it's a field of spread betting with rules of its own and these do take a little getting used to. If you are completely new to financial betting this is probably not where you would choose to strike your first bet.

Taking a position on interest rates involves taking a broad view across a whole spectrum of economic issues. It's important to know, for instance, at what pace the economy is expanding; if growth is stronger than the market believes, this will tend to push up rates; a slowdown has the opposite effect. The current low yields on bonds worldwide reflects expectations that growth is slowing considerably and that inflation has been driven out of the system.

A further major consideration is the state of government finances. A government running a large deficit has to issue paper to fund it and, as with any market, increased supply tends to drive prices lower.

Overseas factors can also play a role. Bond markets compete on a global basis and money can flow from one market to another in search of better returns. Japanese investors, for example, have been heavy buyers of US treasuries for many years now.

Bonds are also considered to enjoy a kind of 'safe haven' quality, and usually benefit when turmoil strikes other markets. If international equity markets ever undergo a serious correction, the ensuing flight to quality would almost certainly send bond prices higher.

And into all this has to be fed the usual capricious mix of market sentiment. Events ranging from statements by central bankers, to stumbles by Boris Yeltsin, can all influence the attitudes of investors.

As with all forms of financial trading, it's important to appreciate the challenges associated with taking a view of these markets. Predicting economic activity and the rate of inflation is exceptionally difficult. Even governments, with all the resources available to them, struggle to get the sort of accuracy they need to shape policy decisions.

A case in point is the problem America's Federal Reserve has had in explaining the paradox of why strong economic growth in the States has not led to rising inflation. Improved productivity through the greater use of new technology is one explanation, but few people believe it's the full story. Fed chairman Alan Greenspan has been known to talk of a mysterious 'factor X', the nature of which remains elusive.

For knowledgeable investors, betting on interest rates offers attractions, but is a complex area and, as always, you need to do your homework before trading.

Section Two

Major markets

5 Betting on commodities

The commodities market, still centred in Chicago but with outposts in New York and London, is perhaps the most intriguing of all financial markets. It's not as characterless or as institutionally driven as the currency or bond markets, and most of us find it easier to relate to an activity where physical goods rather than vague financial instruments are the basis of trade.

This is the market that has touched popular culture more than any other, and having watched Eddie Murphy and Dan Ackroyd attempting to do so in *Trading Places*, most film buffs can usually offer a passable explanation of how you might set about cornering the market in pork bellies.

The truth, of course, is that commodities trading is highly evolved and very sophisticated, and most of the participants are as professional as any currency or bond dealers.

The basic concept underlying commodity markets, as we've seen earlier, is that they provide a regulated market place where producers, traders and consumers of raw materials can buy and sell forward, on margin, and protect themselves against the risk of adverse price movements.

Many of the largest and best-known companies in the world are active in these markets. Oil producers and mining firms, for example, often sell their output forward months, even years before it's left the ground. And food companies may buy coffee, cattle, sugar or orange juice months in advance to protect their margins. And ultimately, because of the stability in prices that all this activity brings about, we, the consumers, reap the benefits.

But that's enough of a eulogy to the market. Whatever about the basic function of commodities trading, the vast bulk of the action is purely speculative. The volatility of prices, combined with the chance to short a market and the ability to trade on margin, draws in many investors with no higher motive than to turn a quick profit. And there's nothing wrong with that.

The variety of contracts traded in places like Chicago and London is vast, and the spread firms price up more than three dozen different markets. But broadly speaking, commodities can be broken down into three occasionally over-lapping categories depending on whether they are agricultural products, industrial raw materials, or precious metals.

Agricultural commodities include those famous pork bellies, grain, corn, orange juice, several varieties of coffee, potatoes, cocoa and sugar, to name but a few. Prices for many of these can be very volatile

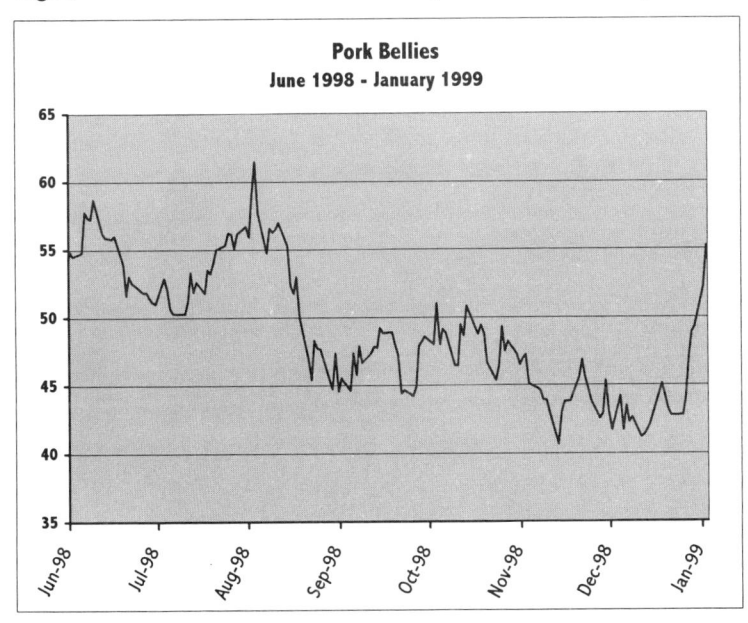

Pork Bellies
June 1998 - January 1999

and attract a lot of keen speculative interest.

The price of any product is a function of supply and demand, and it's a feature of agricultural production that supply cannot be turned on or off like a tap. Lead times can extend to 12 months or more, and crops especially are always vulnerable to disease or bad weather.

You may remember those news stories about El Nino last year; its impact threatened to destroy crops throughout Latin America, raising the possibility of shortages of coffee and other regional produce. A phenomenon like this, or even a much less dramatic change in the weather, such as a few nights of bad frost at a key time, can cause commodity players to win or lose fortunes. Should you ever discover a reliable way of making long-term weather forecasts, forget about betting on whether it will snow at Christmas, trade commodities instead.

Industrial commodities include oil and gas, which are traded in several forms, and most metals.

Of all the many different commodities, oil is the one most closely watched in UK, largely because we remain substantial producers, courtesy of the North Sea oilfields.

The most actively traded contract is Brent crude, which acts as the benchmark price for around for two-thirds of the world's internationally traded crude oil.

Trading in Brent futures takes place on London's International Petroleum Exchange. The IPE is Europe's largest energy exchange and gets through about $1 billion in turnover every day. Brent futures account for about 70 per cent of this.

The oil price has been in the doldrums for some time and is currently trading at 12-year lows. The cause is two-fold. To some extent the slowdown in the world economy has dampened demand. But the main problem is on the supply side. OPEC no longer exerts the sort of pressure it once did on prices, and producer nations are basically just going it alone.

The weather can also have an impact on oil prices, at least in the short-term. A cold snap across Europe or the US can boost demand and push prices higher.

Brent Crude 1998

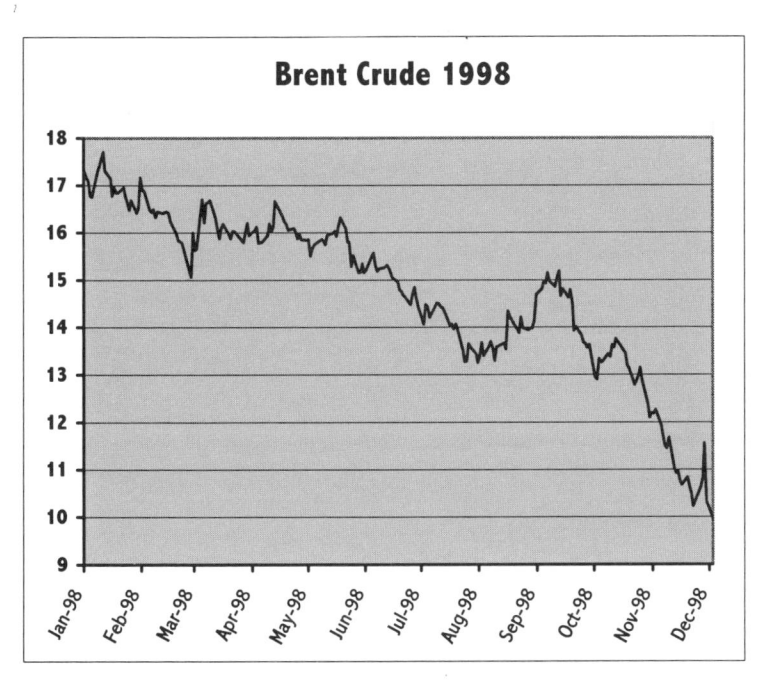

[Chart showing Brent Crude oil prices from Jan-98 to Dec-98, declining from around 17 to about 10]

Longer-term, climate change may also be an issue. The notion of global warming does seem to have some basis in fact – hardly good news for the fossil fuel industry.

Instinctively, we often tend to feel that when prices are at historic lows the next move must be up, but that may not be the case with oil. Unless there is some disruption in the Gulf, or a major recovery in the world economy, it's hard to see where any support may come from.

Aside from oil and gas, the other big industrial commodities are the metals. Copper, tin, lead, zinc and aluminium are all actively traded on the London Metal Exchange. Prices tend to be less volatile than for softer commodities, but there can be significant short-term moves, for instance when an industrial dispute breaks out.

Metals trading is something of a law unto itself. Floor trading, which takes place from 11.45 in the morning and from 3.20 in the afternoon, consists of a series of 'Rings'. These are five-minute spells, where each metal is traded in turn. When the Rings have finished, official so-called 'Kerb' trading begins. This is a period where all the metals can be traded simultaneously. Kerb trading normally runs from 1.15 to

58 . Market Speculating

1.30 at the end of the morning session, and from 4.35 to 5.00 in the afternoon. Trading in the morning session is used for settlement purposes and it's at this time that official prices are fixed.

The best time to deal is when the markets are most liquid. This is usually during a Ring for whichever metal you're interested in, or during one of the official Kerb sessions. Your dealing handbook should list the Ring times for the different metals.

A further catch with the metals market is that settlement dates are not constant, they roll forward. A three-month metal contract quoted on March 5 will have a different settlement date to a three-month contract quoted a couple of weeks later. This is not the case with other commodities, where the March contract will have the same settlement date regardless of when you trade it.

This has important consequences. If you trade three-month copper today, you cannot close the position in a week's time simply by trading three-month copper again, because the settlement dates will have rolled forward and the bets will not be the same. Instead, you need to close the bet for the same date as you opened it. And the price you are offered, because of technical supply and demand issues, may not match the three-month price being quoted in the market.

This may seem a little complicated, and frankly it is. You need to be sure you know what's involved before trading.

As with oil prices, metals have been very weak in recent years. Again, healthy supply combined with the effect of a slowing world economy has taken its toll on prices right across the board. And there may be even worse to come. Producers are always reluctant to cut output in response to falling demand. Generally they prefer to build up stocks, because it's expensive to take facilities off-line, and the hope is always that a rival will cut production first. The futures market, ironically, may also be a contributor to the problem. Many producers will have sold their output forward at prices much higher than today's, so they have little incentive to cut supply.

Commodities prices overall are now at 20-year lows, and they may not recover until the world economy again experiences decent levels of growth and until inventories have been run down.

And, of course, metals and other raw materials are the primary source of wealth in many emerging nations. Continued weakness in commodities prices hinders the prospects for these countries, a factor to be borne in mind when weighing the outlook for the world economy in general.

The final class of commodities is the precious metals: gold, platinum and silver. They each have industrial uses. Platinum, for example, is used in catalytic converters. But these metals are also regarded as having some sort of investment status, and gold in particular has long been perceived as a store of value.

Like most commodities, the precious metals have suffered in recent years, though economic factors have been less of an influence than shifting attitudes on the part of investors.

The idea of holding gold and other physical assets may have made sense 50 years ago when financial markets were less developed than they are today, but the logic is wearing thin. Gold pays no interest, unlike bonds and equities. In fact it actually costs money to hold it because there are storage and insurance costs to be paid.

It's not surprising, then, that central banks have been questioning the

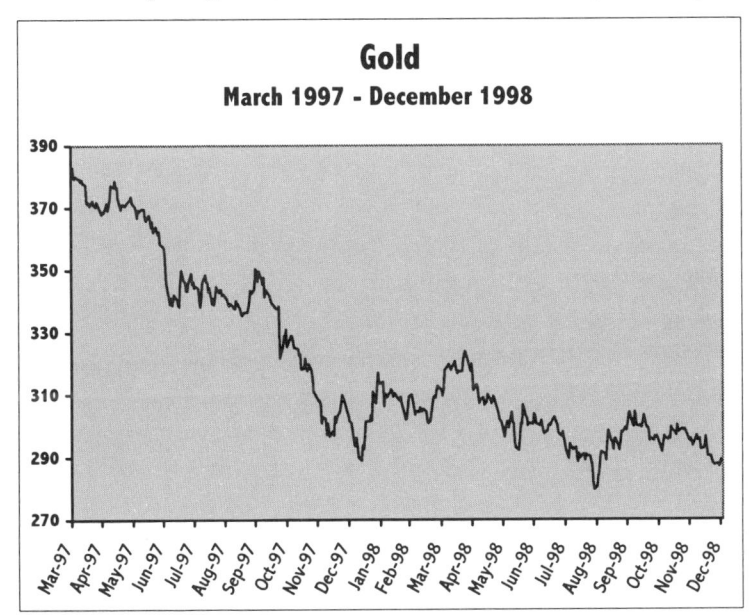

Gold
March 1997 - December 1998

wisdom of holding their reserves in the form of an unproductive yellow metal, and many have been quietly selling into the market. And the central banks have a lot to sell. The Bank of England alone has about £4 billion-worth of the stuff.

This is not to say that gold will never have its day again. If equity markets crumble, or if something nasty were to happen in the Middle East, or even in Asia, gold's defensive qualities might come through once more. Gold bulls might also point out that the opportunity cost of holding precious metals right now has seldom been lower, given that the yields on other assets are so poor.

Commodity trading offers many opportunities to the private investor, but it can be a complex area. You need to understand the markets you're dealing in, and you need to be aware of the pitfalls. Some exchanges, for example, limit price movements and you can find yourself trapped in a deteriorating position with no immediate way of closing out. So it's vital to set stakes at a sensible level and to make appropriate use of controlled risk strategies.

Commodity trading is bigger business in America than it is here. Many US investors trade the markets regularly, almost always adopting a chart-led approach, encouraged by brokers who have the freedom to advertise more aggressively than their counterparts on this side of the Atlantic do.

US investors probably over-trade commodities. The fact that basic raw materials are being dealt in, as opposed to complex financial instruments, does not lessen the degree of expertise needed to make a profit. Late last year the regulator of commodities trading in the States, the Commodity Futures Trading Commission, took the unusual step of warning consumers to beware of brokers promising quick profits with little risk. The CFTC was particularly concerned that investors were trying to make money speculating on obvious seasonal changes. In other words, don't go buying Brent crude in April just because summer's coming and demand for heating fuel is likely to fall. Such things are always factored into the price.

One of the benefits of the American love affair with pork bellies and the rest is that many excellent books on commodities trading have been published there, and if you want to learn more about this area of investing, there's an abundance of specialist literature available.

If the Yanks are perhaps a bit too fond of commodities, the reverse is probably true over here. Most investors scarcely ever consider trading these sorts of futures, and when they do, their thoughts rarely stretch far beyond the outlook for gold. Only one spread bet in 50 is on commodities, and in many cases the customer concerned has a professional connection with the market he or she is trading. These markets do have their challenges, but for those willing to invest the time, opportunities do present themselves and the more experienced spread trader should certainly make the effort to learn more about how these markets work.

62 . Market Speculating

Section Three

Section Three

Options

Options trading is one of the fastest growing forms of financial spread betting. It's also one of the most complex and interesting fields in investment finance.

The options market is a paradox. On one level everything is incredibly simple. The basics can be mastered in a few minutes. Most investors are capable of making intelligent trading decisions after perhaps a few hours of study. Some of the details, though, particularly in the area of pricing, are incredibly complex - the stuff of Nobel prizes, in fact.

The number of investors who use options is still relatively small, but increasing all the time. Awareness of how options work is growing, and more and more of us are being attracted by the way in which certain strategies can be used to combine the same upside potential of a futures bet, but with only a fraction of the risk. And you don't need a PhD in physics to appreciate why that's an appealing proposition.

So what is an option? It's a contract, a financial instrument that gives you the right, but not the obligation, to buy or sell a security at a fixed price on a specified date.

The fixed price in question is known as the strike price. The specified date is called the expiration date.

The fact that the holder of an option is not obliged to use, or 'exercise' it, is important. If a bet works out, you can cash it in, possibly making a great deal of money because options are just as highly leveraged as a futures transaction. But if the option goes wrong, most of the time you're free to walk away, losing nothing more than your original investment.

Private investors are most familiar with equity options. These are options on the shares of major companies, such as HSBC, Shell or Tesco. But the options market is much broader than this.

These days it's possible to trade just about anything, including currencies, commodities and interest rates. The fastest growing field of all concerns stock market index options, with many investors preferring options trades on the FTSE or S&P 500 to much riskier bets on the futures market.

For betting purposes, there are two kinds of options, calls and puts.

A call option gives you the right to buy a security, and it's a bet that the market will rise.

A put option gives you the right to sell, and it's a bet that the market will fall.

Options are tradable and can be bought and sold just like futures. So it's possible to turn a profit or cut a loss long before expiration.

In order to avoid any confusion with the strike price, the market price of an option is often known as the premium.

Obviously, when you trade with a spread firm, no options actually change hands – you are betting on price changes and nothing else. With that in mind, let's consider some scenarios to see how options work in practice.

Suppose shares in company X are trading at £10. You believe the market will move higher and you want to back that view with an options strategy. The simplest method is to buy calls.

A range of strike prices is always available. You might be able to choose from calls with strike prices of £9, £9.50, £10, £10.50, and so on.

A call with a strike price below the market price is said to be 'in the money'. A call with a strike price higher than the market price is 'out of the money'.

In the money options tend to be expensive. They have an intrinsic value because they have already reached the price at which they can be exercised. Out of the money options are usually much cheaper and

66 . Market Speculating

they tend to appeal to investors who want to stake a smaller amount on a high-risk proposition.

Let's say you decide to buy £11 calls, expiring in two months' time. The premium is, say, 50p. You buy 1,000 options with a total value of £500, and that's the most you can lose.

If the share price of company X does not rise to £11, the options are worthless. After all, there is no point in exercising an option and buying a share at £11 if you can buy the same share on the stock market for less.

Between £11 and £11.50, it is worth exercising the options, but the profits don't cover the 50p premium.

Only if the share price moves above £11.50 will the trade actually register a net profit. If the share price at expiry is, say, £12.50, the gain would be £1,000, or a 200 per cent return on the original £500 investment.

A put option would work the other way. Again, assuming a £10 share price, a £9 put expiring in a couple of months' time might cost 40p. Anyone buying a £9 put would not exercise it unless the share price expired below £9. Between £8.60 and £9, the option would be worth exercising, but it would not cover the premium. Only if the share price slumps below £8.60 is a profit made. If it fell to, say, £7.50, a buyer of a thousand £9 puts at 40p each would make £1,100.

As you can see, the appeal of buying puts and calls is that you can win a large amount of money – in the case of call, a theoretically unlimited amount – for a relatively small outlay that is absolutely fixed in value. Whatever happens, you cannot lose a penny more than your original stake. Contrast this with, for example, buying or selling FTSE futures where, if things go wrong, the losses can just keep mounting and mounting.

But, of course, there has to be a catch. If there weren't, no-one would ever trade FTSE futures, would they?

In all financial markets, risk and reward tend to balance out. This is one of the unwritten laws of the financial universe.

The lower risks associated with options trading tend to be reflected in the premium. In other words, buying options is expensive. A small move in the riskier futures market can be enough to make you a profit, but you need a much bigger move on an options trade to finish in front.

As well as buying options, it's also possible to sell them through a process known as 'writing'.

Let's say company X is still trading at £10. You expect the price to rise, but this time instead of buying calls, you opt to sell puts instead.

The £9 put is still trading at 40p, and you sell 1,000 of them. The buyer of those options pays you the premium, a total of £400. This is the most you can win.

If the shares continue to trade above £9, you keep all of the £400. Below £9, you continue to make an ever-diminishing profit down to a price of £8.60. Below this level, you lose money. If the share price collapses to, say, £6, you would lose £2,600.

The attraction of selling is that you get to collect that rich premium from buyers. However, again, risk and reward balance out. The price you pay for that premium is the assumption of a much higher level of risk. The potential profits, not the potential losses, are capped, and you may lose far more than you stand to win.

Selling calls in particular can be extremely risky, especially in the sort of fevered bull market we've seen recently.

Suppose you think that £10 share price will fall. Instead of buying puts, you decide to write calls. This time you sell a thousand £11 calls at 50p each. You pocket £500 in premium and this is as much as you can make on the deal.

If the price holds below £11, you keep all the money. As the price rises from £11 to £11.50 your profits dwindle to nothing. Above £11.50, you lose. Suppose, to take an extreme example, the share price doubles to £20, something that could happen in the event of a takeover bid or in response to an earnings report. You would lose – wait for it - £8,500. And that on a trade where you could never make more than £500.

Most calls are written 'naked'; in other words, the person writing the options doesn't own the shares he's selling. If the option is subsequently exercised, he has to go into the market and buy enough shares to complete the deal.

Some investors, though, write 'covered' calls. This is when you sell calls on shares you already own, and it's actually a low-risk strategy. If the share price rises sharply, you make bigger gains on the shares you own than you lose on the options trade; though, of course, you would have made far more money had you not written the calls at all. Large investors regard writing covered calls as a way of boosting returns in a market that's moving sideways or rising very slowly.

Selling options is risky. And not just in theory. Prior to the '87 crash, many heavyweight investors were writing put options on a large scale. Month after month, in a strongly rising market, it must have seemed like money for old rope. Remember, if you sell puts you only lose money if values fall sharply. Eventually that was exactly what happened and some people lost fortunes.

However tempting it may seem, it's no use accumulating lots of small gains on high-risk transactions, if you give it all back and then some when a market reverses.

Let's summarise the risk profile associated with different option plays:

	Market Rises	**Market Falls**
Buy Calls	Unlimited profits	Losses limited to premium
Buy Puts	Losses limited to premium	Large potential profits
Sell Calls	Unlimited losses	Profits limited to premium
Sell Puts	Profit limited to premium	Large potential losses

In the real world, serious options players often employ quite elaborate strategies involving combination trades. They might open a string of positions in puts and calls at different strike prices to try to profit from a very precise view of where the market's heading. These techniques rejoice in such names as butterflies, condors, boxes, strangles and so on.

One old favourite is a strategy called the straddle.

From time to time, classified ads appear in the business sections of the Sunday papers promising, for a large fee of course, to show you how to make a profit regardless of whether the market rises or falls. What's on sale, I imagine, is an explanation of how straddles work.

Not that you would ever be dumb enough to reply, but let me save you some money and tell you what a straddle is.

A straddle involves simultaneously buying matching put and call options at the same strike price. Betting that the market will rise, and simultaneously betting that it will fall is not as contradictory a position as it may seem.

For example, shares in company X are trading at £10. Three-month calls and puts with a strike price of £10 cost £1 each. You buy both.

If the share price moves above £12 (that's the £10 strike price plus the two £1 premiums) you make a profit. If the price falls below £8 (the strike less the two premiums) you also make a profit. However, if the share price stays in a range between £8 and £12, you lose money.

Therein lies the problem with option straddles. Yes, you do make money regardless of whether the market rises or falls, but *only* if it rises or falls a lot.

The technique does have its uses. If a company is about to release its annual report, or if central bankers are meeting to set interest rates, markets can swing sharply when the news is released. It's in circumstances such as these that professionals may consider using a straddle strategy or some variation thereof. For ordinary investors, though, who also have commissions to factor in to the equation, straddles are rarely worth the effort

In fact, for most people, combination strategies are best avoided. This is even more true in the case of spread betting because it's slightly more expensive to bet on options than it is to trade them directly. The best approach is to stick to simple one-bet transactions.

Most spread punters choose to buy calls or puts, depending on whether they expect a market to rise or fall. And, as we've seen, the attraction of this sort of bet is that at worst you can only lose your initial stake. Quite a few spread players, though, are choosing to sell puts and calls. It's riskier, but they are taking the view that premiums are too high and that the value is on their side.

Determining whether options offer value or not is difficult. Options prices are derived from the prices of other investments, which is why options and futures are known as derivatives, and the calculations can be highly technical.

Five different factors influence the price of an option. These are:

- Time to expiration. The more time there is to run, the greater the chances of the desired move in price. The time premium accounts for a large part of any option's value.

- The difference between the strike price and the current market price of the underlying security. The smaller the gap between the strike price and the current market price, the more likely it is that the option will reach its target before the expiration date.

- Volatility. The more volatile the underlying market, the more likely it is that at some point the option will reach its target price.

- Interest rates. As with futures, the price has to reflect the financing costs of the transaction.

- Dividends. An investor owning equity options foregoes the right to dividends and this has to be allowed for in the price.

In 1973, a couple of American academics called Fisher Black and Myron Scholes published a model that combined all these factors. Today the Black-Scholes model is still regarded as the standard method for calculating the theoretical value of options. Professional traders use off-the-shelf computerised versions of it and feed in whatever data they need.

In 1997, Myron Scholes and Robert Miller picked up the Nobel Prize in economics for further work on the model.

As you might imagine, this is complex stuff. Those City 'rocket scientists' that you sometimes read about in the press, armed with their advanced degrees in physics and maths, often specialise in this area. Which is not to say that they necessarily have a better trading record than the rest of us.

Long Term Capital Management, the hedge fund that nearly went bust in 1998, was supposed to be a low-risk investment vehicle using sophisticated techniques to exploit tiny discrepancies in prices between different markets. Unfortunately the rocket science didn't get off the ground and LTCM had to be bailed out by the banks to the tune of $3.5 billion.

Market prices do not always conform to theory, of course, but most options prices trade somewhere around their theoretically correct values. As a private investor it's not something you need to lose sleep over. Basically, if you feel the underlying market is worth buying or selling, the same should be true of the relevant options. Though bear in mind that the moves have to be quite large for options to be cost-effective.

The most variable element in an option's price is volatility. Volatility is measured in terms of standard deviation. What matters is not how a market has behaved in the past, but how volatile it's expected to be in the future. By feeding all the other elements into the model, including the current market price of the option, it's possible to calculate what's known as implied volatility.

Unlike the other determinants of an option's value, such as time to expiry or interest rates, volatility is not some external value that can be measured objectively. It's a product of the ebb and flow of the market and it fluctuates constantly.

The higher volatility is, the more expensive options become. Volatility will be usually be highest for a company just before results are announced, or if bid rumours are circulating. Currency or interest rate options may become more expensive when important economic data is set to be released. The temptation may be to trade options when there is this sort of obvious potential for dramatic moves in price, but this possibility is always reflected in higher premiums.

For much of the past 12 months, following the Asia crisis and the Russian default, volatilities generally have been extremely high in many markets and this has pushed up the price of options.

It could well be that one reason why so many spread punters have been selling options recently is that they believe volatilities will decline from the high levels we've seen of late, pushing down the value of options right across the board.

So where does all this leave someone using spread bets to trade the options market?

Well, there are probably three broad points worth making.

First, unless you really are an expert – and by that I mean someone working in the market – it's probably best to forget about complex combination trades. Options are expensive and it's very hard for smaller investors to overcome the high dealing costs associated with running multiple positions. It's also best, particularly in the early stages, to stick to buying options rather than selling them. It's less risky.

Secondly, only trade if you think there's a genuine chance of a big move in your favour. A modest move in price will rarely be enough to make an options trade profitable. If you expect a small or gradual move, but you are confident of it, a futures bet would make much more sense. Don't ever be tempted to buy options purely because they are less risky than futures. Remember that there are other methods you can use to manage the risks associated with futures trading.

Thirdly, timing is critical. Every day that passes diminishes the value of an option. It's not enough to expect a big move in a market, ideally you want that move to happen fast. Using options to bet on small movements in the market over an extended period of time is the spread betting equivalent of death by a thousand cuts.

Let me give you an example of a real-world situation where an options strategy might have made sense in the past, and where it might still make sense today.

Many spread punters have been extremely bearish about Wall Street for a long time. The spread firms have told me that, whatever the level, there have always been more sellers than buyers of the US market.

Most of these investors have used futures and, as the market is currently at an all-time high, they have all lost money, in some cases a great deal of it. And yet, though stock markets worldwide have risen sharply since autumn '98, there is still a school of thought that shares are significantly over-valued and that any correction could be sharp and prolonged.

Here's a situation where buying puts would make sense. There is the possibility of a significant move, one that could develop very quickly.

But calling a top is notoriously difficult and the market might just keep powering ahead, which makes selling futures too risky for most investors.

So for bears, perhaps the best approach would be to buy puts that are well out of the money. They are cheap, the potential losses are capped, but if the market reverses in a significant way, the upside is considerable.

Not everyone would agree with this approach, but the fact is, had Wall Street sellers used options in this way rather than futures, they would have suffered much lower losses than they have, but would still have profited had the market moved in their favour.

Options trading is the most complex form of financial spread betting. Even so, simple options strategies are not hard to understand and they have a place in every investor's toolbox. If you want to learn more, there are many books published on the subject. Better still, the spread firms occasionally organise open evenings and seminars and these provide a great opportunity to ask questions and discuss some of the trickier aspects of options trading.

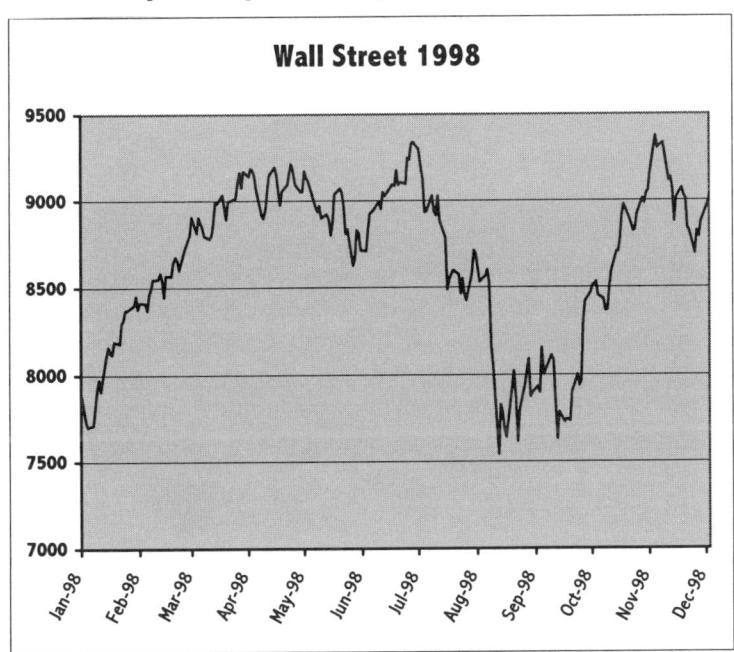

Wall Street 1998

74 . Market Speculating

Section Four

Section Four

Trading strategies

1 Managing risk

Risk means different things to different people.

In the eyes of most investors risk has powerful, negative connotations. Risk relates to the possibility of incurring a loss and it must be minimised, even eliminated, wherever possible.

That's a healthy view, and anyone with memories of a bet or investment gone badly wrong will sympathise with the attitude. But it's not the full story.

Risk and reward

You may know that the Chinese pictogram for the word 'crisis' is composed of two separate characters that symbolise 'threat' and 'opportunity'.

Risk is like that.

It's double-edged. It can work in our favour just as readily as it can work against us. It delivers unexpected windfalls with as much indifference as it hits us with those unexpected losses.

When the buyer of currency, bond or equity loses money, a seller somewhere else in the market gains just as much. Risk and reward are intimately bound together. They are two sides of the same coin.

Successful investing is not about eliminating risk. It can't be done.

It's about managing, or controlling risk, in the hope that eventually that fine balance between risk and reward tilts in our favour. And getting that balance right is not easy.

Risk-management

First off, let's be clear: spread betting is inherently risky. It's hard to succeed at it and many people who try, fail. There are steps that can be taken to keep the dangers in check, but if you are genuinely risk-averse, or if you cannot afford a bet to go wrong, then you should not be trading. It's that simple.

With that financial health warning out of the way, there are really two aspects to handling the risks associated with spread betting.

The firms themselves like to point to a selection of techniques or devices that can be used to put a floor under potential losses. These methods are important. Every investor should be intimately acquainted with them and should probably use one or other most of the time. But it's also important to understand that these techniques, which we'll examine in detail later, provide nothing more than a sort of artificial safety net. They can be a lifesaver when you fall off the highwire, but the essence of risk management is to stop things going wrong in the first place.

To put it at its simplest, the best safeguard you can have is to trade very cautiously, choosing positions with great care and setting stakes with a ruthless eye to the downside.

Before spelling out what this means in practice, it might be a good idea first to clarify precisely what is meant by 'risk' in a financial context.

Defining risk

Although most of us tend to think of risk as a fairly vague, nebulous concept, in the financial markets it has a very well defined meaning. Risk is considered to be synonymous with volatility. In other words, a stable market is said to have a low risk attached to it; a market

78 . Market Speculating

fluctuating wildly is considered to be more risky.

For instance, in the currency markets, sterling and the dollar tend to move broadly in unison. But the dollar and the yen can swing in dramatically different directions. So the pound/dollar rate (or 'cable' as it's known in the trade) is significantly less risky than dollar/yen.

To go a step further, volatility can even be measured and given a precise value. This is done by compiling historical price data and calculating the standard deviation.

Just as volatilities are calculated for individual currencies and shares, similar calculations can be made for entire markets. Comparing how individual shares move in relation to the stock market, for example, gives rise to what are known as beta values.

A share with a beta of 1.0 moves perfectly in line with the market. It would, on average, rise ten per cent when the market rises ten per cent, and so on. British Airways, for example, has a beta just above 1.0.

Many retailers, like WH Smith and Boots, have betas of about 0.5. When the market rises or falls by ten per cent, typically they fall or rise by only five per cent.

Unpredictable businesses, such as biotech stocks, can have betas greater than 2.0. And some sectors can even have negative betas, moving in the opposite direction of the wider market. This has been true of certain oils stocks lately.

Publications like the *Investors' Chronicle* often include betas when listing company details.

This may seem somewhat technical and it's hardly the stuff of bar room conversation, but betas can have surprising relevance for ordinary investors.

You may notice, for example, that those large fund management companies – the ones with the huge ads in the weekend press – always seem to be trumpeting some fund or other that's beating the market, irrespective of whether the market is going up or down.

Does this mean that you should immediately send all your money to these genius fund managers so that they can handle your investments for you? No, because behind the hype lies a simple act of financial sleight of hand.

Fund management companies typically run a complete array of funds. If they have any sense, they ensure that at least one has a high beta value, which means it will out-perform in a rising market. But they also make sure to run a low beta fund, which will out-perform when the market's falling. This way they always have something seemingly impressive to advertise.

But when all the funds are added together, in total, they generally fail to match the market. That's why if you ever do decide to use a collective investment vehicle, your best bet is not some expensive flagship fund with a well-known face at the helm, but an anonymous low-cost tracker fund that mirrors movement in a major index such as the FTSE-100.

Volatility and staking

When trading, it's not essential to have precise betas and volatilities to hand, though anyone betting on individual shares might like to know what they are, if only for the sake of completeness. It is important, however, to have at least a broad sense of the volatility of any market you may be about to trade. Charts help, but most experienced investors develop a feel for particular markets.

Volatility is not something that exists in isolation: it has to be related to stakes. The two should always match. A seemingly risky market can be safe to trade if the stakes are low enough and if a prudent stop-loss is used. But even the dullest commodity or interest rate play can be lethal if that predictability encourages you to drop your guard and you push your stakes beyond a sensible level.

I'm sure there's a dictionary somewhere that defines an optimist as someone who spread bets regularly. Every time you trade, at least initially, you expect to make money. No-one would open a position otherwise. The danger is, though, that this optimism can seduce you into focusing more on the upside potential of a bet than on the downside. The result can be over-staking. This is a tendency every investor should guard against. In fact most of us would probably die richer if we always staked just a little bit less than we felt we should.

Screening

Good risk control is as much about the bets you don't have as the bets you do. The difference between success and failure often has as much to do with screening out bad trades as it does with backing winners.

Every time you prepare to deal, it's worth running through certain questions. Is the trade-off between risk and reward acceptable? Is the stake right? Is there a better way to back this view? Why am I trading – is there a good reason why I'm right and the market's wrong? Is there a chance of a better trade tomorrow? Should I wait? Should I trade at all?

It's hard to make money spread betting. It's hard to pit your wits against a major financial market, pay the spread, and win. It's important to respect the challenges that exist.

It may not always seem that way, but avoiding an average loser has as much of an impact on your bank balance as backing an average winner. Always remember that the best way to manage risk is to back as few losers as possible.

Risk-control techniques

All trades have the potential to go wrong. In conventional betting terms, if you go to the racecourse and somehow contrive to back an even-money shot at 10-1, it's a great bet, but you would still lose your money 50 per cent of the time. It's the same in the financial markets. No matter how clever you are, no matter how carefully and skilfully you trade, there is always the danger that a position will turn sour, and you need to be prepared for it.

For most people, small losses are not a problem. Such knocks are reluctantly accepted as part and parcel of speculative trading. The real danger is of a position going badly wrong. When it happens, given the unlimited nature of many spread bets, the consequences can be extreme. It's this sort of threat that any sensible investor must guard against.

Fortunately there are three specific techniques that can be used to put a floor under potential losses. These are stop-loss orders, controlled risk bets, and options trades.

Each method is slightly different, with its own advantages and limitations. Most investors should use one of these techniques most of the time. Inexperienced spread traders and those with very limited risk capital should employ these safeguards all the time.

Stop-loss orders

The most widely used risk-management technique in spread betting, and in all financial markets, is the stop-loss order.

The spread firms will accept instructions to trade if the market reaches a certain level. This can be used to open a position, but more commonly it's used as a device to cap losses.

For example, let's say you buy £10 of December FTSE at 6300, but you don't want to risk any more than £1,000 on the position. When opening the trade you could instruct the dealer to place a stop at 6200. If the quotation falls to this level, the position should be closed and you won't lose any more than £1,000.

It's important to realise that what triggers the stop is the bookmaker's quote, not the futures market and certainly not the cash market. And therein lies the first problem with stop-losses, which is that you are at the mercy of how the bookmaker prices his market. You may not even know that the stop has been executed.

Stops are usually put in place when the position is being opened, but they can be requested subsequently. They can also be changed, so if your view of the market alters, or if you are keen to lock in a profit, the stop can be tightened up.

The great drawback with stop-losses is that they offer no guarantees. A stop-loss is an order to trade at a given level, but market conditions may not make it possible to trade at that level. Some markets can move very quickly, particularly if an unexpected event has taken place, such as a shock move in interest rates. Technical breaks on a chart can also have an impact, with many stop-losses in the market set at similar levels.

There are plenty of instances of this happening. On occasions

82 . Market Speculating

dollar/yen has seen large step-moves, and equity markets, especially in the US, are as volatile as they have ever been.

When a market moves suddenly, the spread firms will execute stops at the best levels they can, but that may still leave investors with bigger losses than they expected.

The different spread firms may apply stop-losses in different ways, and it's essential to study the trading manuals and familiarise yourself with the rules of the firm you're dealing with.

IG Index, for instance, treats stop orders and other instructions as completely separate transactions. There is no automatic link between a stop and the open position it relates to. So if you close out a position, you must also explicitly cancel any stop that applies to it, otherwise the stop could still be executed and you might find yourself getting a contract note through the post for a deal you never intended to make.

In addition, there are costs associated with handling stop-losses, and as a result the spread firms may raise the minimum bet size for clients who want to take advantage of this facility.

To their credit, the firms try to keep customers informed and if a

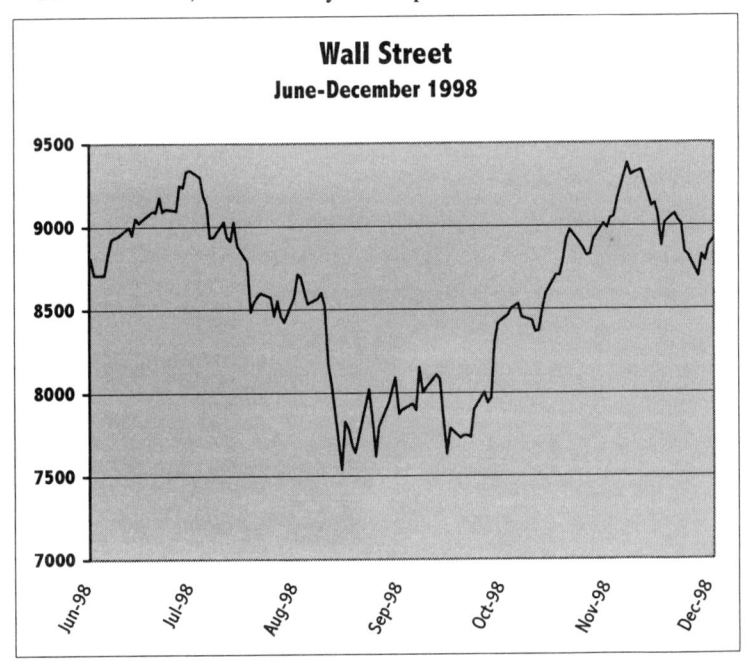

Wall Street
June-December 1998

stop is reached, a dealer will probably give you a call to let you know the order has been executed.

When it comes to setting stop-losses, there are basically two approaches. Some investors have a more or less fixed idea of how much they are prepared to lose on a trade, and they use that as a limit.

The more advanced approach is to use technical analysis. Typically this involves studying the charts, identifying resistance and support levels, and fixing stop-losses to offer protection should these levels be breached.

This is how most professionals work, particularly in the currency markets, where so much of the trading is technically driven. The danger with this approach is that everyone is looking at the same charts and that, right across the market, orders tends to be placed at very similar levels. This can lead to sharp price movements when technical levels are broken.

As a rule, the shorter your time horizons, the more aware you need to be of technical considerations. If you take a longer, more fundamental view, it's easier to rise above the daily fluctuations and general noise of the market.

One of the indirect benefits of using a stop-loss is that it imposes a certain discipline on the way you trade. If you have no target at all, losses on a bad bet can quickly run out of control. And the problem with purely mental stop-losses is that it's too easy not to carry them out. I can certainly think of instances where I've held on to positions longer than I should, hoping the market would turn. Committing to a firm stop-loss every time you trade is a good habit to get into.

Controlled-risk bets

The spread firms do not like to see customers losing a lot of money. This may seem hard to believe, but it's true.

When a client suffers a heavy loss, not only do the spread firms face immediate problems getting the cash in but, much more importantly, it may also be a long time before that client feels confident enough to trade again. And, of course, if one customer burns his fingers, perhaps because of a sharp move in the stock market, the likelihood is that many others will have done the same.

This is what happened during the '87 crash. Many people lost a great deal of money at the time, but the real problem for the spread firms was that turnover plummeted. In the aftermath of the crash, many investors simply refused to trade. It took the then emerging spread betting industry literally years to recover fully.

Since then the spread firms have been very mindful to educate their clients about risk, and new ways have been sought to protect investors against the worst extremes of the markets.

One of the best innovations is the controlled risk bet.

This is a bet with a built in stop-loss. The critical difference, though, is that unlike conventional stops, this time the level is guaranteed. Even if the market drives straight through the stop-loss, the bet is closed at the agreed limit.

What happens with a controlled risk bet, in effect, is that the spread firm, rather than the client, assumes the risk. In return, the spreads on a controlled risk bet are higher. In volatile markets, though, a few extra points can be a small price for the extra security.

As with more conventional stop-losses, one drawback with controlled risk bets is that they are triggered not by the level of the underlying market, but by the mid-point of the spread. A position can be closed out without your knowing it, though a dealer will usually try to call and confirm this.

Also, controlled risk bets are risky for the bookmakers. As a consequence they are not available across every market. For instance, there are no controlled risk bets on traded options. Index Direct offers a narrower range of bets, all of which have limited risk.

Controlled risk bets tend to be favoured by smaller, more risk-averse investors, but professionals have been known to take advantage of them under certain circumstances.

Just after the Iraqi invasion of Kuwait, for example, as tension in the region mounted, IG Index laid a Middle Eastern gentleman a very large controlled risk bet that the price of oil would rise. As operation Desert Storm got under, with the usual perversity of financial markets, the crude price promptly went into freefall. All the bad news, it seemed, had been discounted in the price. IG collected, but the client would have lost a fortune had he not traded on a controlled risk basis.

Options

The final technique for limiting risk involves trading options - or to be more precise - buying them, because, as we've seen, selling options exposes investors to just as much risk as futures trading.

Suppose you are bullish about the London stock market and want to buy. You could choose FTSE futures, using a controlled risk bet or a conventional stop-loss order to limit the potential losses.

An alternative would be to buy a call option. If the FTSE were trading at 6000, an option with a strike price of 6200 and with three months left to run would trade with a mid-point in a range somewhere between 250 and 300. If you were to buy £10 at, say, 280 the most you could lose on the position would be £2,800.

Calls further out of the money (i.e. those with even higher strike prices) would cost less. The most you could lose on a 6400 call, for instance, might be 200 points. But the cheaper the option, the further the market would have to rise for you to show a profit.

The main drawback with options is that they just aren't suitable for betting on small or gradual moves in the market. In such circumstances, futures are more cost-effective.

Options in general seem to be under-exploited by spread punters, and not just because they are a good way of limiting risk. As the spread industry evolves and continues to grow, interest in options trading looks sure to rise.

Section Four

Trading strategies

2 Getting through the early months

After opening a spread betting account for the first time, it's only natural to want to get down to business as soon as possible. No-one, though, should ever be in a rush to start trading.

Those stiff warnings that the regulators insist on having plastered all over the brochures and advertisements are there for a reason. Spread betting is risky. It's possible to lose a great deal of money very quickly, and it is a form of trading that's certainly not suitable for every kind of investor.

Those risks never go away. Financial folklore is littered with cautionary tales of highly qualified people losing control, playing fast and loose with the markets, and eventually reaping the consequences.

Nick Leeson, you may recall, was regarded as a star trader in Singapore until he started chasing losses on Japanese Nikkei futures in 1995, running up a bill of £830 million and bringing down Barings Bank in the process. It's still mind-boggling to think that a major financial institution could give one young man on the far side of the world enough unchecked power to inflict such extraordinary damage.

The Barings fiasco remains the most dramatic example of how experienced professionals can get things wrong, but similar instances happen all the time, it's just that the amounts involved are smaller so the stories tend to be less widely reported in the media.

Already this year at least two futures firms have been shut down by the SFA following huge losses incurred by individual clients. In one case a professional futures trader blew £6 million speculating on German interest rates. The client of another, much smaller firm dropped £500,000 trading Dax futures. Neither man could meet his liabilities.

It's possible to make a lot of money trading the financial markets. And it's worth bearing in mind that whilst Nick Leeson was losing a billion pounds, other traders elsewhere in the market were taking it off him. But when experienced, highly paid experts like these can get things so catastrophically wrong, it's a clear sign that private investors should be very respectful of the challenges involved in making the game pay.

This is particularly true in the first few months of trading. Experience counts for so much, and it is easy to get things wrong whilst negotiating those first few trades. This is a time when novice investors should be less concerned with making money and more concerned simply with surviving.

Anyone who can battle their way through this tough period, build up some experience, develop a feel for the markets, and master the technicalities of trading, should find profits a little easier to come by in the future.

There are certain basic steps that everyone should consider taking, not just during the early stages, but even before the first bet has been struck.

Learn all you can

We all learn from our mistakes. But mistakes can come at a high price, especially in the financial markets. It cost Nick Leeson, for example, a billion pounds and a prison sentence to learn that chasing losses is not a good idea.

Trial and error will always feature in a trader's education, but there are less brutal ways to learn. It makes a great deal of sense to work hard and to make the effort to learn as much as possible by other means.

For a start, make sure you understand the details of how a market works before you trade it. This may seem blindingly obvious, but novice traders are often so enthusiastic that as soon as a potential opportunity catches their eye, they skim through the relevant passage of the dealing handbook and rush into a position before they really understand the implications.

This happens with remarkable frequency. Whilst discussing another issue with a senior dealer, he told me in exasperation how, on that one afternoon alone, he had been forced to explain the workings of a market to two separate clients, both of whom had already placed bets and were wondering why things were not going as they expected.

Always make sure you know the rules. Reading the dealing handbooks helps, but these do not contain all the answers. If you have any doubts, speak to a dealer before trading and make sure everything is crystal clear before putting any money on the line.

Knowing how markets work is vital, but it's only the starting point. The next step is to learn more about what moves markets. Read the financial press. Listen to and watch the business reports on radio and television. Though be warned: the level of coverage outside the specialist media tends to be too superficial to be of much direct value.

It's also worth reading one or two books on futures trading. Most of the best titles are American; our US cousins seem to have a more populist attitude towards investing than is the case over here. Some of the better titles currently in print are listed in Appendix One.

If you have access to the Internet, there are many good sites worth visiting, though again most are aimed at American investors.

Many of the big investment banks and brokerages have their own sites and frequently post quite detailed research and other reports. By the time these reach a website they may be a little out of date, but it's a very good way for private investors to get a sense of how the big players are thinking. And, of course, the great thing about the Internet is that all of this is free. It's a terrific source of information, including up-to-date charts and so on, and investors will rely on it more and more in the future. Appendix Two highlights a number of websites that are worth a look.

In addition to all this information, there is a lot of knowledge out there that has never been written down. Experience is the best teacher, but it doesn't have to be your own experience. If possible, it's always a good idea to speak to other investors who have been futures trading or spread betting for a while. They have usually learned a great deal through experience and you can often save yourself a ridiculous amount of money simply by heeding what they have to say.

For example, many of the spread traders I've spoken to only really came to appreciate the importance of stop-losses once they had been badly stung on an early position that ran badly out of control. Collectively, private investors have probably spent millions of pounds learning the hard way how to control risk. Don't make that sum any greater than it is already.

The spread firms often organise seminars and open evenings, and these provide a good opportunity for newcomers to hear the war stories and inspect the battle scars of more experienced traders.

Simulation

One of the principal ways in which professional traders are now taught to do their job is through the use of sophisticated computer programs designed to simulate a real trading environment.

Novice investors might consider trying a similar approach. Before committing any hard cash, try opening and closing a few imaginary positions to see how it works out. Select realistic stakes and use actual quotes from the spread firms. Prices are available on-line, but if you ring up, just ask for an 'indication', which is a quick guide-price for someone not intending to trade immediately.

Clearly this is not the same as trading with real money. The whole emotional aspect of dealing – the greed and the fear – is removed from the equation. It's easier to be bold when there's no price to be paid for getting things wrong, and there's no problem letting a position run when you are not fixated on the minute-by-minute gyrations of the market.

Despite the obvious lack of limitations, many lessons can still be learned from simulated trading, particularly for an investor who has no other kind of experience. It can help to drive home just how volatile markets are and how important it is to get the staking right. And it often serves to highlight just how tough it is to make steady profits over any period of time.

Everyone should make the effort to spend a few weeks 'trading' in this manner before moving on to real bets.

This approach costs nothing and there are no risks attached, so it's cheaper to learn even the smallest lesson this way than it is to learn the same lesson a few weeks later when a possibly significant amount of money may be on the line.

Start small

There is only one right way to start trading, and that's to start as small and as cautiously as possible.

It's hard to make money spread betting. Experienced traders, including those who work in the City, find it hard to win consistently. It's common sense for a newcomer, who may never have traded before, to start warily and to assume that, at least initially, many bets will simply not work out.

Until you have some worthwhile experience under your belt, and until you have settled on a pattern of trading that seems to work fairly reliably, keep the stakes small and bet very selectively.

In the past this was impossible for most people to do. The minimum stakes on many markets were pitched so high that it was relatively easy to lose a thousand pounds or more in an afternoon. There really was no way to start small. In fact, many people may have suffered excessively heavy losses on one or two poor early trades and been forced out of spread betting as a result. They were put out of the game before they had a chance to progress further along the learning curve.

Thankfully it's different today. There are still no small spread bets – even £2 a point on the FTSE can mean £500 won or lost in a day, albeit on rare occasions. But at least it's possible for someone new to spread betting, and without a mountain of capital, to start betting, and to start learning, without being knocked out of action the first time a bet goes badly wrong.

When choosing stakes, we all tend to focus on what we might win rather than on what we stand to lose, and as a result most of us have a tendency to stake a little more aggressively than we should. It's important to keep this instinct under control. Those of you new to spread betting should make a resolution that, come what may, the first five or six bets you place will all be at minimum stakes. Better still, if you have the self-discipline and can pull it off, continue to trade at minimum stakes indefinitely. Only increase the stakes once it becomes clear that it would be profitable to do so.

Remember that there's no hurry. The financial markets will always be there, and there will always be something to bet on. This race is a marathon not a sprint. It's better to get things right gradually and realistically than to rush in, all fired up with enthusiasm, only to fizzle out disappointed and quite a bit poorer six weeks later.

Start small. Learn your lessons when it is relatively cheap to learn them. Keep as much capital intact as possible. And only increase stakes when it makes sense to do so.

Risk control

Perhaps the one thing that inexperienced traders get wrong more than any other is that they fail to pay proper attention to risk management.

It's as if, somehow, none of us can really take the issue seriously until we've had one big trade of our own go into meltdown.

Maybe it's that optimism thing again. We expect to win every time we bet. After all, we wouldn't bet otherwise. So although we can read about risk control, and hear other people's horror stories, like the proverbial road accident, on some deep level we always expect the victim to be someone else.

Well, here is a harsh but true fact: accidents do not always happen to other people. If you do not manage risk properly, it can only ever be a matter of time before you suffer the consequences.

Without doubt, everyone new to spread betting should use one of the various risk-limiting techniques every time they trade. It's that simple.

In addition, it's also important to be prepared to take a loss sooner rather than later. When things start to go wrong, the temptation is always to hang on and to hope that something will turn up. Sometimes it will. More often than not, though, things just go from bad to worse. A stop-loss is the last line of defence, nothing more, and no-one should ever hesitate to close out a position quickly once it starts to turn sour.

Again, if you speak to experienced traders, most of them have painful memories of heavy losses that could have been trimmed to almost nothing if a bad trade had been closed out as soon as it started to go wrong.

In the early months at least, it is always better to take losses too quickly rather than too slowly. If you find that most losing bets are running right down to the limit and are being stopped out, then you are probably not closing out quickly enough. Remember, in the early stages it's as much about preserving capital as it is about making money, and that's hard to do if every losing bet is inflicting real damage.

Section Four

Trading strategies

3 Technical analysis I: An introduction to charting

Where most private investors are concerned, trading decisions are usually the product of a complex mix of factors, including fundamental analysis, technical analysis and, in many cases, nothing more concrete than an intuitive feel for the market.

In a sense, fundamental analysis should matter most. Fundamental forces are those that have a direct impact on an underlying investment.

Changes in exchange rates, for example, are driven ultimately by such basic economic factors as growth, interest rate differentials, the balance of payments, inflation, and so on. The eventual fate of equity markets is prey to these same influences, as well as to the outlook for corporate profits, levels of company taxation, take-over activity and so on.

But these elements, powerful though they may be, take time to assert themselves. Most traders, on the other hand, almost by definition, have their eyes fixed on much shorter time horizons.

Though they can be, and sometimes are used in such a way, spread bets are not really long-term tools. Most positions are opened and closed within a couple of weeks. This shifts the balance away from fundamental analysis towards methods that have more predictive value in the short-run, and this is why most traders pay special attention to technical indicators.

94 . Market Speculating

This is not to say that the fundamentals don't matter. Far from it. They tend to win out in the end, even if the end can be a long time coming. What's more, market perceptions of the fundamental outlook can shift very rapidly, so long-term forces can have very dramatic near-term consequences.

A couple of years ago, for instance, much media attention was focused on the supposed miracle that was the Asian Tiger economies. A stream of politicians, academics and commentators trooped off to the Far East in search of lessons to be learnt. Yet, 12 months later, talk of Asian Tigers had given way to panic about an Asian Crisis, and the only Westerners trooping off to the region were economists dispatched by the IMF.

It took a while for the fundamentals to exert their relentless gravitational effect, but they did; and though the forces at work, such as over-valued currencies, were long-term in nature, the market reaction to the crisis was sharp and very rapid.

The moral is that fundamental analysis cannot be ignored.

Even so, it's technical considerations that tend to have the upper hand in short-term trading. Technical factors are those that relate to the markets themselves, rather than to any underlying investments.

The study of charts is the best-known but by no means only form of technical analysis. Other elements added to the mix include funds flow, analysis of so-called 'market internals' and the use of leading indicators.

Not everyone is a huge fan of technical analysis, and certainly there are aspects of it that have about as much credibility as *feng shui*. Indeed, some investors in America make trading decisions based on horoscopes. Others swear that the result of the Super Bowl in January determines the direction of Wall Street for the rest of the year. Still, what can you expect from a country where one in ten don't believe in evolution.

The serious purpose of technical analysis is to deliver insights into market behaviour. After all, in the short-run it's this behaviour, even more so than the performance of underlying investments, that traders are trying to predict.

Charts

For as long as there have been markets, investors have studied charts in an attempt to spot trends that might give an indication of what will happen in the future.

Charting has always been a slightly controversial discipline. It can sometimes be hard to see what the connection is between last month's price action and the events shaping today's market environment.

To take an exaggerated example, a bullish three-month chart formation for company X is not a lot of use if, out in the real world, the same company is preparing to issue a profits warning.

And yet, charts matter. They matter because the price of a security more than any other measure reflects what is known about that security.

If a company really were about to issue a profits warning, for example, you might well see some advance weakness in the share price, because certain market participants would inevitably get wind of the bad news ahead of time and seek to profit from it.

And this is not dry academic theory. Again and again, out in the real world, share prices regularly pre-empt the release of market-sensitive information.

Charts also matter because they provide us with a visual representation of market psychology.

Investors do not behave randomly, even if it occasionally seems that way. In the market, a herd instinct tends to prevail; and that herd behaves in similar ways under similar circumstances, and the recurring patterns show up in the charts.

Finally – and this point cannot be understated – charts have relevance because investors *think* they have relevance.

In areas such as short-term futures trading and in the currency markets, practically every serious participant will have a chart at his or her elbow. All these charts will be identical, and though there's always scope for interpretation, virtually everyone will have the same trendlines and indicators pencilled in and will plan their trading accordingly. The widespread use of charts has more than the touch of the self-fulfilling prophecy about it.

Trendlines

The most basic and most reliable charting technique involves determining simple trendlines. These are lines that connect a series of highs or lows within a trend. Such lines can offer either support or resistance to a market.

Support is a level the market can reach but not fall below. Resistance is a level the market can reach but not rise above.

The space between resistance and support is called a channel.

In the example table below the market is in a slight upward trend. Downtrends are equally possible. If the trendlines are horizontal the market is said to be consolidating.

Once a trend becomes apparent there are several ways to try to profit from it. One option is simply to trade the broad direction of the market, taking a long view and waiting for the fluctuations to cancel themselves out. This would involve running a medium-term position, probably to low stakes, and with a generous stop-loss.

Other investors might try to play the range, buying when the market dips towards support and selling when it rises towards resistance.

It is possible to have a whole series of trends prevailing all at the

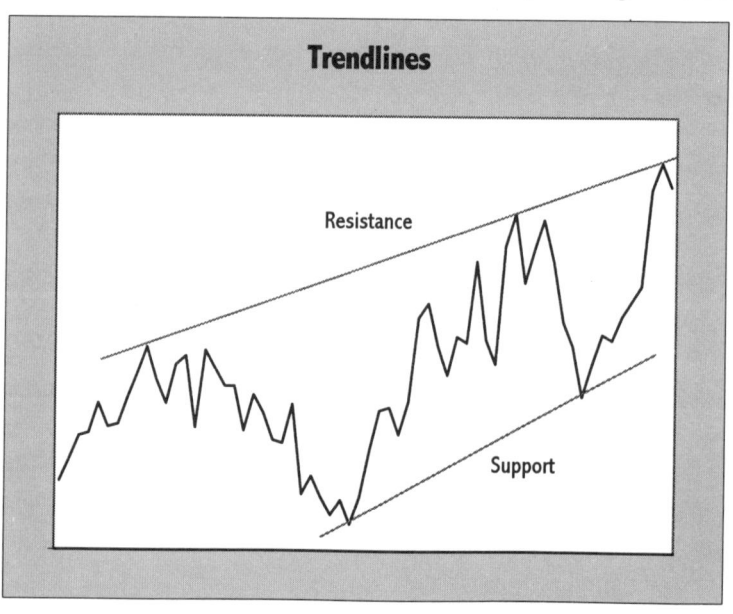

Trends within trends

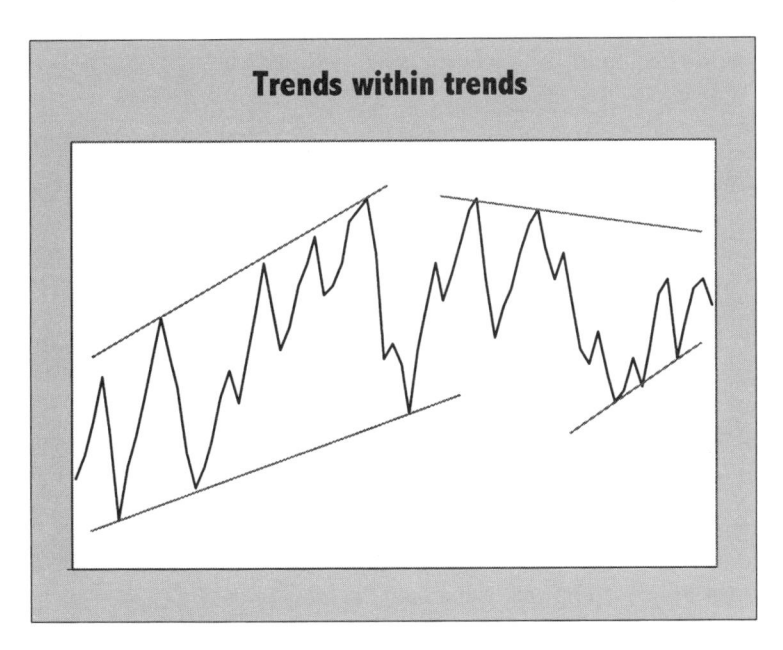

same time. Long-term trends often contain shorter-term trends, each with their own resistance and support levels (see above illustration).

The significance attached to different support and resistance levels can vary. Generally, the longer a trend has been in place, the more important it is.

It may sound a statement of the obvious, but chartists maintain that trends are intact until they are broken.

A breakout occurs when the market moves outside a trend channel, and it's usually accompanied by a significant move in price. When this happens, if the market rises above a resistance line, that level then becomes a support. If the market falls below a support, that line then becomes a resistance.

Some traders will actually buy a market when it moves very close to the top of its range, and sell as it approaches support. The idea is that if the trendlines are broken, the market might make a substantial move in the trader's favour. This sort of tactic requires the setting of tight stop-losses in case the established trendlines hold firm.

Another feature to watch for is a gap in the charts. This happens when, for example, the market opens at a higher level than it closed the day before. Chart gaps are often associated with new trends and sharp moves in price.

A further way to identify trends and to highlight potential turning points is to use moving averages.

Normally short- and long-term moving averages are used in combination, with the short-run average intended as a lead indicator of a change to the longer-term trend.

The choice of which moving averages to use depends very much on the time scale over which you intend to trade. Longer-term investors may combine MA's of 40 and 200 working days. This is probably too long a measure to be of practical value to active spread traders, though it might help to put short-term trends into longer-term perspective.

For shorter–term trading, MA's of 10, 15 or 30 days can be useful. If you have the software available, it's sometimes worth experimenting with different averages and testing to see which is most accurately matching the market.

Very short-term traders, those jobbing in and out during the course of a day, need to focus on even tighter micro-trends, and they will often rely on 15-minute MA's to guide them.

Whatever time scale you trade to, as they say in the markets, the trend is your friend. That gem is probably every bit as simplistic as it sounds, but it's certainly the case that most professional traders prefer to ride trends rather than to buck them.

Retracements

Not even the most clearly established trends produce markets that move in one direction for long. A stock market rising or even, God help us, falling for more than three or four days running is usually considered worthy of mention.

The standard pattern across most markets is for a move in one direction to be followed by a retracement, which is a smaller move back in the opposite direction.

Retracements are hugely important and reading them accurately is vital for successful trading.

A great deal of effort has gone in to trying predict how far retracements are likely to run once underway.

The most widely used indicators are Fibonacci ratios. According to these, a move is most likely to end after retracing 61.8 per cent, 38.2 per cent or 50 per cent of the previous move. These levels are marked in on many charts as soon as a retracement starts to become apparent.

You may well ask why a move should reverse at 60 per cent, let alone at 61.8 per cent.

You can pin the blame on Leonardo Fibonacci, an Italian mathematician who lived around 1200AD. He bequeathed us the sequence of numbers that bears his name, in which each number is the sum of the two previous numbers, 0,1,1,2,3,5,8,13,21 and so on.

The most important ratio buried away in this sequence is the so-called Golden Mean, which, after skipping the first few digits, is the ratio between any two successive numbers in the sequence. It averages out at 61.8 per cent and it's a ratio with a surprising degree of relevance across many disciplines. We know that the ancient Greeks and the Egyptians knew about it, and it crops up repeatedly in music, biology and architecture; as well, of course, as in the dealing rooms of the City.

It's hard to offer any convincing explanation for why retracements should fizzle out at 38.2 per cent rather than 32.8 per cent, but it does seem to happen. Perhaps this is one of those instances where charts work because investors believe they work.

The popularity of Fibonacci ratios has been encouraged at least in part by a school of chartism known as Elliott Wave Theory, after one Ralph Nelson Elliott who published details of his methodology in 1939.

Elliott believed that market moves consisted of a rising 'impulse wave' of five parts, followed by a corrective wave usually of three parts, with the relationships between them determined by various rules, including the use of Fibonacci numbers.

Elliott was an optimist who believed that down moves were always corrective and that new impulse waves always reached new highs eventually.

100 . Market Speculating

Along with WD Gann, Elliott is one of the godfathers of modern technical analysis and you will come across his work if you read further on the subject.

Overbought and oversold conditions

Technical analysts often talk about a market being overbought or oversold.

Overbought conditions exist when prices have risen too steeply too fast. An oversold situation is where prices have fallen too far too fast. In both cases, the market is likely to react by retracing some of the move.

Complex mathematical tools called oscillators are often used as indicators in this area. Most private investors, though, try to simplify things somewhat. A good method is to establish a trendline for the market using a suitable moving average. If the market diverges from this trend unusually sharply, without a clear reason why, it's a fair bet that prices are moving into overbought or oversold territory.

The temptation then can be to try to anticipate a retracement and to bet against the direction of the market. Such an approach can be very

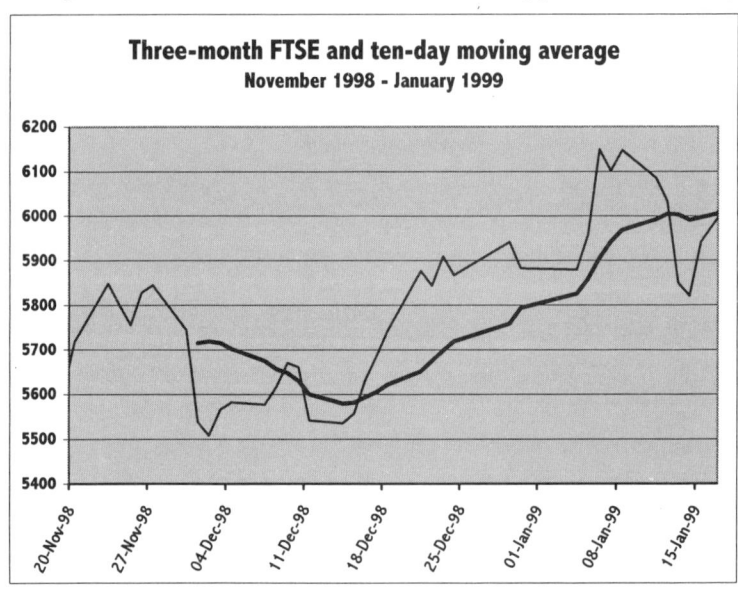

Three-month FTSE and ten-day moving average
November 1998 - January 1999

lucrative when it works. The danger is, though, that overbought or oversold conditions can persist, even deepen, for a long time before prices return to more normal levels.

Successful short-term trading is really not about predicting the market's next step. That's a thankless task at the best of times, particularly for those of us who are not sitting at a dealing desk all day. Instead, success is usually a function of waiting for a worthwhile trend to become apparent and then tagging along for the ride. So if you do believe a market is overbought or oversold, the smart option is probably not to pre-empt a reverse in the market, but to watch and wait and then to trade once a retracement gets underway.

An important concept in this area is that of momentum. Momentum relates to the strength of a market move. When momentum is strong, a move is likely to be sustained. But if momentum is weak, not only may a move fail to hold, but the market could also be at a turning point.

The mathematical calculations used to measure momentum can be quite sophisticated. Many technical analysts will plot changes in the rate at which the market is rising or falling, for instance.

A simpler guide to momentum, and one that anyone can understand, is to study market volume. Moves on the back of good volume tend to be reliable and likely to hold. On the other hand, moves based on thin turnover can be suspect. Volumes for many leading markets are published daily in the *FT*.

Another indicator to watch for is volatility, as reflected in the gap between the market's high and low for the day. A wider than usual trading range can be a warning that there's a tug of war going on between buyers and sellers, and a significant move could follow if one side wins out.

Relative strength

In technical analysis, the term 'relative strength' is used in several contexts.

As far as private investors are concerned, the most important of these involves comparing the performance of a company's share price against that of the relevant stock market sector, or even against the market as a whole.

A share that's outperforming similar shares often continues to do so. It signals buying interest and that investors like the company. Relative weakness suggests the opposite.

Relative strength is a technique used by many professional stock market investors as a way of fine-tuning timing decisions. They may feel that certain companies are under-valued but, even if that opinion is correct, it can take months or years before the market comes round to a similar point of view. Rather than buying and holding, these investors wait until relative strength indicators show that the company is coming into fashion and then they move in. This is part of the reason why good relative strength tends to be self-reinforcing.

In order for an indicator to be as reliable as possible, it's important to compare apples with apples and to judge a company in relation to its competitors. Broader comparisons with the wider market can be misleading. For example, an oil company rising against the market, but not against its own sector, might have more to do with changes in the price of crude than with stronger underlying demand on the part of investors.

Chart patterns

In addition to pinpointing trends, technical analysts also look for patterns in the charts.

The theory is that certain common shapes map out the collective psychology of investors, and that well-established patterns of behaviour re-assert themselves whenever similar circumstances arise.

One of the most common formations, with a certain relevance today, is the double top.

A double top arises when the market hits a peak, then sells off, then rallies to the original high, then sells off again (see illustration).

The interest in this particular formation arises because the London and New York markets may be in the process of tracing out just such a pattern right now.

Double Top

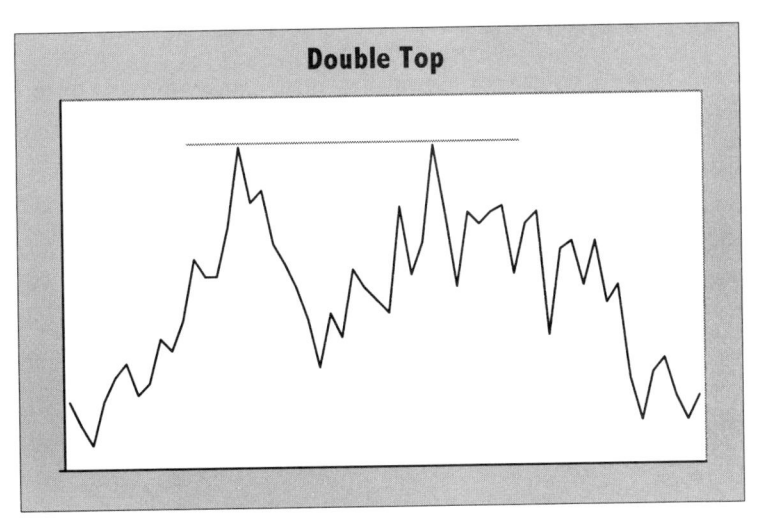

This is quite unlikely, though. A classic double top is more than just a couple of consecutive highs at similar levels. For the formation to be complete, following the second peak, the market must sell-off down through the level from which it rallied. Conventional wisdom holds that once this support is broken, the market should fall a further 20 per cent. As you can imagine, this makes double tops one of the most bearish patterns possible.

True double tops, though, are quite rare. In order for Wall Street to trace out a legitimate double top, for instance, the index would have to break back down below 7400, and at the moment that looks a long way away.

The reverse of the double top is the double bottom, and it's regarded as an equally powerful signal to buy.

Triple tops and bottoms, though very rare indeed, are also possible. They are just extended versions of the same thing.

Another popular pattern analysts watch for is the head and shoulders formation. This pattern develops over time when a market makes a series of three peaks. The tops of the outer peaks (the shoulders) must be at roughly the same level, and the top of the inner peak (the head) must be higher than the other two peaks (see illustration overleaf).

A head and shoulders formation is considered to be bearish if the price dips below the shoulder line.

Head and Shoulders

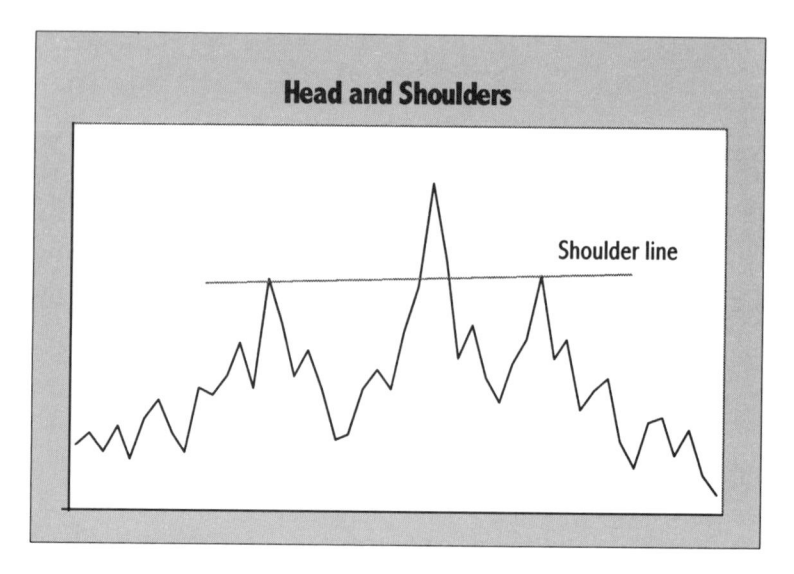

[Chart showing Head and Shoulders pattern with Shoulder line]

A reverse head and shoulders, formed by three dips, with the middle dip lower than the outer two, is bullish if the market breaks above the shoulder line.

Other chart patterns such as flags, pennants and triangles are also picked up on analysts' radar.

It's worth remembering when looking for formations such as these that it's not a tidy mathematical exercise. As someone once put it, you set about the task with a crayon, not a ruler and pencil.

Once traced out, these popular formations can lead to sharp moves in the market. Anticipating this, some investors like to launch pre-emptive strikes, opening positions even before the patterns are complete. This can work, but the danger is that the market angles off in the wrong direction at the last minute. So if you do try to get on early and beat the rush, maintain a tight stop-loss just in case things don't work out.

Advanced techniques

Charting can become as complex as you want it to be. For one thing, you can graduate onto ever more elaborate ways of expressing the price data.

Rising market / Falling market

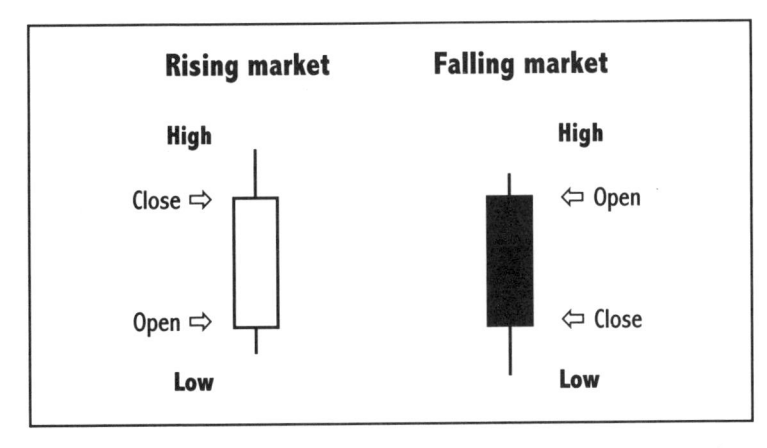

Rising market
- High
- Close ⇨
- Open ⇨
- Low

Falling market
- High
- ⇦ Open
- ⇦ Close
- Low

One technique is to use Japanese Candlesticks. This is an ancient form of analysis that plots the day's high and low on a single line called the shadow, with the difference between the day's opening and closing price represented by a narrow rectangle called the body. If the market closed higher than it opened, the body is white. If the market closed lower than it opened, the body is shaded:

Candlestick charts feature their own special patterns, usually given appropriately oriental names.

The very latest charting techniques, though, are more dependent on RAM's and CPU's than on shadows and bodies. Professional investors are harnessing ever-more sophisticated computing technology in an attempt to unlock the hidden secrets buried away in yesterday's price action.

Cutting edge technical analysis increasingly involves the use of computers with artificial intelligence, which is to say, systems designed to mimic the processes of the human brain; and also neural networks, which are AI programs capable of 'learning' through a process of trial and error.

The prospect of taking on market professionals and institutions armed with such technology may seem intimidating, but the value of such systems has yet to be proved. Besides, computerised trading is based on the notion of trying to make tiny percentage profits on huge trading volume. Private investors play a very different game, trading much more selectively and aiming for higher returns as a result.

Using charts in practice

Investors need to use charts intelligently. Charts provide a reliable guide to general trends. They also indicate key support, resistance and retracement levels. Knowledge of these can help you time your trades better.

For example, you haven't known pain until you've bought a market near the top, just before a correction gets underway, and then been forced to close out at a much lower level just as the market turns and rallies to a new high. An awareness of major support and resistance levels can help avoid such bloodshed.

Identifying major chart levels can also be valuable when setting stop-loss and, in particular, controlled risk limits.

For example, if you buy the FTSE at 6200 and know that there is very strong support at, say, 6080, it would be smart to set a controlled risk limit at around 6075. If 6080 were to give way, you would be fully protected against the possibility of the market moving sharply and suddenly against you.

The great appeal of charts is that, though they are open to interpretation, they provide objective answers. But it's important to understand that these answers come with no guarantees.

A chart may give the most unequivocal buying signal, yet prices may tumble.

An investor struggling to finalise a trading decision often finds himself trapped in a state of unresolved mental conflict, torn between all manner of contradictory signals. The danger then becomes that we can be tempted to put more faith than we should in charts because they can provide such simple, unambiguous answers.

Charts offer signs and guidance, nothing more than that. Never subordinate your own sense of judgement to a handful of lines on a page.

Both the weakness and the strength of charts reside in the fact that they are used universally by so many people across so many markets. It's a weakness because widely available information tends to be discounted and is normally reflected in prices ahead of time. It's a strength because in the financial markets perception creates its own reality. The herd-like instincts of most investors is such that if something is believed to be true, it may as well be true.

The bottom line is that charts exert a real influence on the market and you have to heed the signals. But don't ever expect to get rich just from reading the runes.

Section Four

Trading strategies

4 Technical analysis II: Beyond charts

The use of charts is the most widely recognised aspect of technical analysis, but there are also other techniques and considerations that fall into this category. Some of these have limited value and some are absolutely critical. Knowledge of what the Americans call 'market internals', for example, can help you to spot turning points in the market and to time your trades. Broader issues, such as an awareness of the supply and demand pressures weighing on prices, can point you towards profitable positions and steer you clear of riskier ones.

Supply and demand

Just about the first lesson that anyone ever learns in economics is that, in the absence of outside intervention, prices – all prices – are determined by an equilibrium between supply and demand. It's no different in the financial markets. We can study price/earnings ratios, dividend yields, purchasing power parity, and any other valuation benchmark you could care to mention, but ultimately prices gravitate towards that point at which supply and demand connect.

Supply is obviously one half of the equation, but in the financial markets supply is usually either semi-fixed, or slow to respond. The supply of companies on the stock market, for example, tends to be more or less constant, at least in the short-run. The same is true for the supply of currencies and bonds. So as far as short-term pressures are concerned, most of the impact emanates from the demand side.

Tracking fluctuations in demand is not that difficult. The dominant players in all financial markets are the big institutions - the pension funds, the insurance companies, the unit trusts, open-ended investment companies, and so on. And if you know the strength of their revenues and the amount of cash they happen to be holding, it's not hard to get a sense of the build-up in demand for equities in particular.

The data available in America tends to be more comprehensive and accessible than it is on this side of the Atlantic, and for those tracking it, it's painted a remarkable picture in recent years.

The flow of cash into US mutual funds, which are collective investment vehicles similar to unit trusts, has been relentless. At times, private investors have been pumping a billion dollars a day into the market.

According to the Investment Company Institute, a Washington-based organisation that monitors institutional funds flow, in the first six months of 1998, over $126 billion poured into these funds.

For quite a long time now, many experts have struggled to find a really convincing explanation for why the US stock market has continued to defy conventional valuation yardsticks and just kept on hitting new highs. There's been discussion about low inflation, higher productivity through the greater use of new technology, and mutterings about all sorts of 'new paradigms'. But perhaps the single best explanation for the lofty heights being reached on Wall Street is that there's just more and more money chasing basically the same number of shares. In such circumstances there's really only one way valuations can go.

The incredible extremes in price that can result when rampaging demand collides head on with more or less fixed supply is demonstrated best of all in the Internet sector.

Many people take the view that the principal commercial platform in the medium-term future will be the Internet. Investors are desperate for

110 . Market Speculating

exposure to the sector. But the supply of even halfway suitable companies is tiny. In the US, the market value of tradable Internet shares, in other words those shares that are up for grabs and not already owned by company directors, is about $40 billion. That may sound a lot but, in current market conditions, it's nothing. The entire tradable Internet sector is worth less than McDonalds. The result is stratospheric price movements. Last year in the US, the average Internet-related new issues rose by over 100 per cent. Shares in Amazon.com, the star of the sector, rose six-fold.

This explosion in demand for shares on both sides of the Atlantic has been fuelled by a combination of factors. Demographics have played a big part. Populations in the West are ageing, and as people age they save more. Also, governments have made it clear that in the future the state is going to bear less and less of the burden of providing for peoples' retirement. And as state pension provision has been eroded, investors are having the sense to put more and more aside themselves.

All of this has happened at a time when conventional wisdom asserts that the stock market is the best place for investors to put their money. This perception may break down in the future but it's certainly

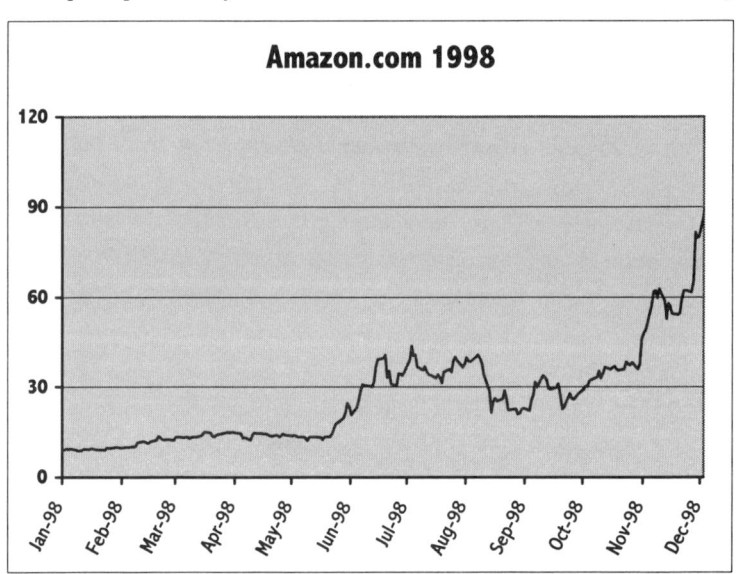

Amazon.com 1998

underpinning liquidity at the moment. And, of course, the relentless bull market of recent years has had a certain self-sustaining quality to it; the better shares perform, the keener investors are to commit whatever new money they have to the market.

Appreciating the strength of demand is important. As mentioned previously, many spread traders have sold Wall Street aggressively over recent years. But sellers are likely to remain frustrated, not to say poorer, so long as the flow of funds continues to be so strong. Demand is an indicator that every trader must watch closely because it has such a powerful and direct bearing on price levels.

Interestingly, there are possible signs that the flood of money into US mutual funds has started to abate recently. One provisional figure released as we went to press suggested that 1999 actually started with a small cash outflow.

Bears might want to keep those claws sharp. Certainly in the US, investors are just about as exposed to the market as they can be. Americans now have more wealth tied up in shares than they do in their own homes. If Wall Street were to go into a serious downturn, those same individuals who have propelled the market higher might opt to cash in and run for the exits. If they did, the same torrent of liquidity that has magnified moves on the upside could exert just as big an influence in the opposite direction. If shares really start to reverse, they could do sharply and quickly. Sellers may yet have their day.

Monitoring shifts in supply and demand is not limited to the equity markets, though it becomes trickier in other areas because it's harder for private investors to get their hands on reliable data.

The currency markets are intriguing. Supply and demand are critical because so much of the trading is technically driven, prompted by speculation and not by any underlying economic activity. The hedge funds run by the likes of George Soros provide much of the liquidity, though they have had their wings clipped recently following the near collapse of Long Term Capital Management last year.

Hedge funds are risk-taking, speculatively orientated investment vehicles that are targeted at wealthy individuals. Some funds won't accept an investment below $100,000. Almost all hedge funds are registered in anonymous, barely regulated offshore havens.

The amounts of money under control are not huge in absolute terms. Soros' flagship Quantum fund has around $10 billion under management. But hedge funds are free to borrow money and to take on risky, highly leveraged positions. When LTCM flirted with disaster last year, $3.5 billion was needed to bail it out, but its exposure to the markets was far higher than that. Had it been allowed to fail, the fear was that it would have wreaked havoc throughout the financial system. All the banks are so tightly bound together that if a bankrupt hedge fund were to drag one or two banks down along with it, the rest would topple like so many dominoes.

Like John Meriwether who ran LTCM, Soros has had his bad days too. His funds lost $400 million in minutes when the dollar collapsed overnight against the yen last year. And Russia's default cost the Soros funds $2 billion in a matter of days.

The impact of the hedge funds on the currency markets is considerable but there is no real way for private investors to get a sense of what is going on. The fact that hedge funds are all registered in offshore havens means that they can keep their positions secret from just about everyone, including the regulators. Investment banks will often deal with hedge funds on virtually no profit margins just to try to gain an insight into how the funds are positioning themselves. The fact that private investors are excluded from playing this sort game is just one of the handicaps we face when trying to outwit the market professionals.

Fortunately for us, not all participants in the currency markets get to operate in such an environment of secrecy. Central banks are often active in the market, particularly when a currency is under speculative attack. In the short-term, the banks can conceal their activities. But eventually they have to publish the levels of their foreign reserves. If these reserves have fallen or risen significantly, it's usually an indicator of intervention. Though a central bank can shore up a currency for a while, the market usually gets its way eventually; after all, central banks can't intervene forever.

Clear-cut instances of major currencies being mis-aligned are rare, but when they do arise, as with sterling in 1992, thanks to spread betting smaller investors can make money just as easily as George Soros.

The hardest area of all in which to judge supply and demand trends is in the commodities market. Private investors are at an almost insurmountable disadvantage compared to some of the larger corporate players.

Take a product like coffee. The international food companies who process and distribute it have access to an extraordinary volume of market intelligence. They can measure and predict demand better than anyone else. But it doesn't stop there. They will also take steps to secure supply-side data. In many cases, for instance, they will hire people in the appropriate regions to go off to conduct crop surveys and to assess the broad overall level of production. Clearly, any private investor hoping to trade profitably against this sort of backdrop needs to tread very warily indeed.

Leading indicators

Many technical analysts pay close attention to certain indicators that are reckoned to foreshadow events elsewhere in the market.

Commodity prices are believed by many to give an early indication of the overall level of activity in the world economy.

The basic logic of this idea is hard to fault. The first place that any changes in growth are likely to be felt is in demand for raw materials. Rather than examining commodities one by one, investors typically look to a broad measure, such as the Bridge-Commodity Research Bureau (CRB) futures index, which trades in New York. Incidentally, the spread firms take bets on it.

If commodity prices really are a reliable pointer, then the world is in serious trouble. The CRB has fallen around 22 per cent in the past three years and there's no sign of a recovery any time soon.

The reality is, though, that commodity prices probably don't predict the future very accurately. Prices are a function not just of industrial demand, but also of supply; and we know that oil producers, to take

CRB Index
June 1998 - January 1999

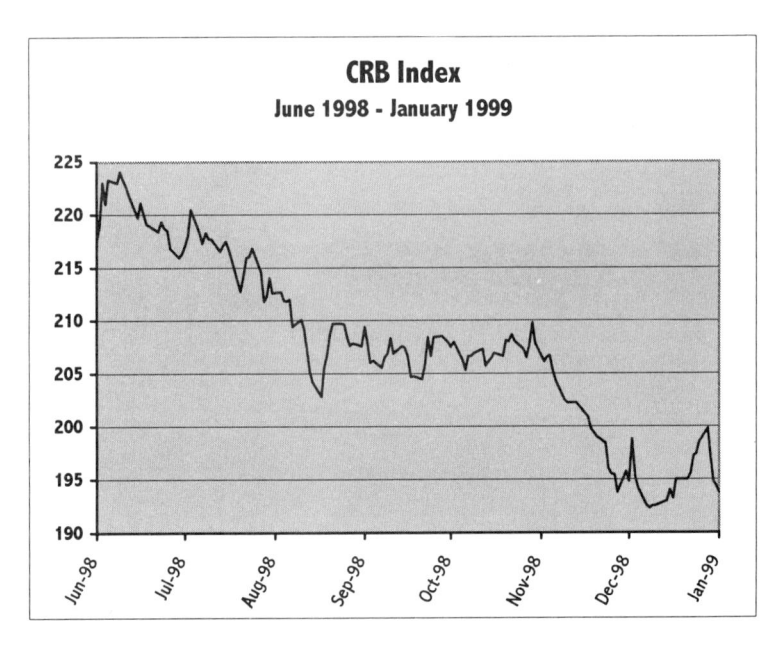

one example, have shown little discipline lately in controlling output. Indeed, producers generally are often reluctant to cut back when a downturn sets in. They may well have sold production forward on the futures market at a good price, leaving them with little incentive to limit output. And even when things get bad, it's expensive to mothball production facilities, so the temptation is always to build up inventories and hope that either demand recovers or that a rival, perhaps with a higher cost-base, will shut down first.

For these reasons, particularly the build-up of inventory when demand slackens, rises in commodity prices may actually lag movements in the global economy.

Besides, the world has moved on. Maybe 20 years ago it made sense to keep an eye on commodity prices, but things are different now. In most developed countries industrial production no longer provides the foundation for all other economic activity. Today, services and knowledge-based industries are far more important. As a serious trading tool, scrutinising commodity prices has little value.

A more reliable guide is to study specific sectors of the stock market that are exposed to levels of activity early in the supply chain. Some traders, for example, keep a close eye on companies involved in transportation and distribution. Any change in the volume of goods being moved around the country is likely to provide a good early signal about the direction of many other parts of the economy.

Other lead indicators that professionals watch out for relate to consumer confidence, which obviously has a direct bearing on the health of the economy, and activity in the housing market, which feeds through later into demand for consumer durables and other goods. Investors betting on interest rates, which tend to be ultra-sensitive to shifts in the outlook for inflation, study employment data, partly because of the implications it can have for wages. They also focus on price date, such as changes in factory gate prices, which can act as a precursor to inflationary pressure at the retail level.

Market internals

Stock market indices are the fairest measures of general stock market performance. That's why we trade them. But indices have their drawbacks. Some are just not very representative. The main Wall Street index, for example, is a very shallow measure of the US market. Its direction can even run against the grain of moves in the wider market, because in times of crisis or uncertainty large, stable multinationals like Coca-Cola and IBM can enjoy a sort of safe haven quality.

Even when an index is broadly representative, such as the S&P 500 or the FTSE-100, that index still paints a very one-dimensional picture. Technical analysts seek further data about the market. By analysing this additional data, the idea is that a more comprehensive picture can be built up and that this may give a more reliable signal to the future direction of the market.

The first statistic to check is volume. Volume is a guide to the underlying strength of the market, and a strong move up or down supported by good volume is likely to be sustained. Conversely, traders need to be cautious about any move on the back of thin turnover. It can happen that up-days are marked by good volume and down days by lower turnover, and this sort of pattern is always regarded as sign of underlying strength in the market, and is a bullish indicator.

Technical analysts also look at the breakdown between the number of issues rising and falling. An index can be distorted by big moves in a relatively small number of larger stocks; this is certainly the case with the FTSE, where pharmaceuticals and other sectors are over-represented. Comparing risers and fallers gives an alternative snapshot of the wider market.

This data is often used to plot what's known as an advance/decline line. This is done by taking the number of risers and fallers on a day, adding or subtracting to get a net figure, and calculating a moving average, usually of around ten days. Many traders regard the direction of the advance/decline line as a good pointer to the short-term direction of the market. This method is more commonly used in the States, where the widely followed, and ominously named, McClellan Summation Index is the best-known form of advance/decline line.

A similar approach can be used to compare the number of shares hitting new highs and new lows on the day. Again, this gives a broader picture of what is going on in the market and it's regarded as a worthwhile indicator.

Sentiment

Sentiment is just another word for the mood of the market. The stock market is rarely driven by anything so predictable as logic, especially in the short-term, and price fluctuations depend as much on how investors feel as on anything else.

Sentiment is an inverse indicator. In other words, the more concerned that investors become about the market, the more likely it is that prices will rise, because whatever bad news is out there should already be reflected in prices. This is why it's often said that a bull market climbs a wall of worry.

Equally, the more enthusiastic that investors become about shares, the greater the risk of a fall in prices, because whatever good news there is has been discounted and investors are already likely to be fully committed to the market.

Sentiment is an abstract concept, so it's hard to measure in any kind of concrete fashion. But there are some technical indicators that you can use. From time to time, surveys are conducted by the financial press into the attitudes of fund managers, and these provide at least a glimpse into the way professionals are thinking.

A more objective yardstick is to take a look at the action in the derivatives markets. If investors are buying more call options than puts, it's a clear sign of bullishness on their part.

A certain degree of caution has to be exercised in interpreting this sort of data, though. Futures and options are often vehicles for hedging, which means they don't necessarily reflect the underlying views of investors. This is particularly the case where put options are concerned, as the investor may just be protecting a long position elsewhere in the market. Heavy purchases of call options and futures, though, tend to suggest that bulls are in the ascendancy. As is often the case, the key is to watch for a trend, and not to over-react to one day's data.

Section Four

Trading strategies

5 Money management

Spread betting is not a game. It's a serious business. If you doubt that, wait until a trade goes wrong and see how much levity you can muster when the margin calls start coming.

To succeed requires a highly disciplined and professional approach, the same sort of approach that the firms themselves employ. Betting casually, without rules and without a plan doesn't work. You can still back winners, particularly when the major markets are rampaging off in a clear direction - as the say in the City, in a strong wind even turkeys can fly - but there's a world of difference between having the occasional good day, and actually making real money over time, which is the goal we should all be working towards.

Central to any trading strategy is a clear, disciplined approach to what's often called money management. Money management refers to how a trader handles his capital, how he allocates it, how he builds it and how he conserves it when things go wrong.

Risk capital

The most basic rule of money management is that you need a float. No-one can really be free to trade properly without a certain amount of risk capital set aside. It doesn't have to be a huge sum. You don't need the resources of a hedge fund, but you do need at least some capital permanently set aside for no other purpose than trading.

In all probability, most spread traders don't even get this far. If they fancy a punt and have some money available, they go ahead and deal and worry about the consequences later.

There are several very good reasons, though, why this sort of casual short-termism hardly ever results in anything other than long-term failure.

It would be nice to think that we could move gracefully from one triumphant trade to the next, but we all know that's not how it works in the real world. No matter how inspired you may be, sometimes things go wrong. That's why all traders need to be able to take a loss. More than that, you need to be almost comfortable taking a loss.

Admittedly, it's hard to show much equanimity when statements start arriving through the post with those wretched prepaid envelopes oh-so-thoughtfully included. But the idea is to develop a strategy, or a pattern of trading, that works for you. And to do this properly you need enough capital so that no one trade, good or bad, will ever be enough to blow you off course.

Trading without sufficient funds creates all kinds of problems. For one thing, if it's all or nothing every time you trade, sooner or later the coin will land on nothing and you're out of the game, at least for a while. And obviously during that time you may miss out on any number of opportunities. It goes without saying that one of the natural laws of spread betting is that all the best chances present themselves three days before payday.

What's more, if you really cannot afford to lose, the danger is that you end up chasing apparent 'sure things' just to avoid a loss.

To take an example, someone might be tempted to buy Wall Street because recent history suggests that there have been many more up days than down. But we all know at the back of our minds that US shares are probably over-valued and that at any point in time there's an outside chance of the market dropping through the floorboards.

Rather than just trying to turn a profit today, often the smarter option is to go for the percentage play, to gamble on a risky position that might go wrong – but which could deliver spectacular gains if things work out. Only those who can afford to bear a little financial pain can accept trade-offs like this.

Also, much as we like to talk in hard rational terms, the fact is that trading is an emotional business.

A certain amount of emotional involvement is unavoidable. We're not fund managers smoking cigars and playing God with other people's savings. It's our own hard-earned, and it would be impossible not to feel a least a degree of anxiety or elation when the market is accelerating off in some direction or another. A little passion is even a good thing because it fuels commitment and it helps to keep us motivated. But if the emotional stakes are too high – which usually happens when the financial stakes are too high – then it can begin to undermine your judgement and the consequences can be disastrous.

Once the ability to analyse a situation objectively starts to slip, all manner of errors can creep in. You may find yourself not taking a profit when you know you should. Worse, you may find yourself riding a position ever deeper into the red, hanging on and hanging on just that little bit longer in the hope the market will turn. Just one bad screw-up like that can wipe out the profits from a whole string of sensibly played, carefully worked out winners.

Spread betting is risky. The stakes are never low. Losing control is dangerous, and though it may be possible to dodge bullets for a while, reckless trading always gets punished in the end.

The bottom line is that you need a bank. If you don't have one yet, start saving. The markets will wait for you. Trust me, they'll still be there in six months' time. In the meantime, you can try placing imaginary trades just to familiarise yourself with the process and to test your reading of the markets. It's not the same as putting real money on the line, but it's still a worthwhile exercise. Resist the urge to take any short cuts. Until you can afford to lose, you cannot afford to trade.

How big should a bank be? Well, it's a matter for debate. It really depends on how you intend to trade. Generally, it's good to think less in terms of absolute cash amounts and more in terms of the number of losing trades you could afford to make.

Let's say you decide that the most you will risk on any one position is £1,000 and that you will use stop-loss orders or controlled risk bets to ensure that this ceiling stays firmly in place. If you have £10,000 set aside, then you have enough for ten trades, and so on.

If you deal very selectively, perhaps once or twice a month, and you stick to less volatile markets, you might get away with having just enough capital to cover five or six trades, at least to begin with. If you trade much more aggressively and favour choppier markets, you might want a float large enough to cover as many as 20 deals or more.

Obviously, although you might be prepared to lose £1,000 on a single trade, you would aim to lose far less than that on an average losing bet.

Once you have settled on the relationship between the amount of risk capital that you have available, and the amount of it that you are prepared to gamble each time, you can adjust the specific sums involved to reflect the impact of any subsequent gains or losses.

So, for instance, if you are comfortable risking a tenth of your capital every time, and a good winner takes the float up to £12,000, you could afford to risk £1200 the next time you traded, and so on. Always bear in mind that it's better to risk too little than too much.

It's a sad but indisputable fact that most spread traders lose money, so until you have enough evidence to prove that you are not amongst them, caution is a virtue.

You may not always feel like risking identical amounts of money on different trades. This is quite reasonable. The degree of value on offer in any given situation will vary, as will your level of confidence. Just try to be broadly consistent. And don't keep kidding yourself that the next deal always warrants higher stakes than usual.

Stakes

If you happen to be new to spread betting, in one important respect, this is the best-ever time to start.

Up until now the spread firms have perhaps not done as much as

122 . Market Speculating

they might to encourage customers to stake sensibly and with restraint. Let's face it, these firms are there to make money, and it's in their interests to have us stake as much as possible every time we trade. Minimum stakes have been pitched at very high levels, particularly given the volatility of financial markets worldwide over the past year or two.

It's been almost impossible for all but the wealthiest spread traders to put in place the sort of prudent money-management techniques that this hazardous discipline demands.

Not so long ago the minimum bet size on the FTSE or on Wall Street was £10 a point. Given that 100-point daily trading ranges on these markets are common, and that swings of 200-300 points are hardly freak occurrences, it's pretty clear that to run a position in these areas requires deep pockets. A bank large enough to accommodate, say ten trades, couldn't weigh in at any less than £20,000.

Most of us just don't have that sort of risk capital. Indeed, people working in the business will admit privately that bets on this sort scale are only really appropriate for customers earning more than about £50,000 year, and even that's probably being conservative.

Fortunately, the spread firms are starting to radically re-think the size of bets they offer.

As you will have noticed, IG Index have sponsored this book and, to be honest, one reason why is because they want to highlight their new Index Direct operation. It offers spread bets with much lower minimum stakes than have been available in the past. The introduction of these lower stakes has to be a good thing. And though IG are leading the way, the other spread firms may well move in the same direction before long.

Now it's possible to play FTSE and Wall Street for £2 a point, and the Far East markets for as little as 50p a point. These modest amounts can still multiply up to a lot of money on a volatile day, or even over a not-so-volatile week, but the sums involved are at least manageable.

This move towards lower staking is partly aimed at broadening out the appeal of spread betting. It's sure to do that. But a secondary benefit for those of us already sold on spread betting is that now we can trade much more comfortably in relation to the capital we have available.

The drawback of betting in smaller sizes is that the spreads are wider. Partly this is due to the fact that it costs the spread firms more to process several small bets than one larger one. It's also the case that there's less competition at the bottom end of the market. If you are betting £10 a point on the FTSE, the spreads are competing with futures contracts. At £2 a point, it's spreads or nothing.

One practical way in which to try to offset the higher margins is to lengthen your time horizons, which is, of course, much easier to do when the stakes are smaller.

Investors risking larger amounts of money normally trade in and out of the market quite quickly, with tight stop-losses, trying to capitalise on small price movements. Though they pay smaller spreads, they also pay those spreads more frequently.

Smaller investors may be in a position, bank permitting, to set looser stop-losses and to ride out the daily fluctuations of the market in the hope of profiting from longer-term trends unfolding over a period of weeks or more.

Closing out

Proper money management isn't just about staking sensibly, though that's a *sine qua non*. It's also about coping with whatever the markets throw at you, and knowing when to run for the exits and when to sit tight.

Conventional wisdom holds that you should always cut your losses and let your profits run.

Then again, conventional wisdom also states that you never go broke taking a profit. Though this is undoubtedly correct factually, it does rather cut against the grain of at least part of the earlier advice.

The truth is that there are no easy answers. The financial markets are complex, dynamic and unpredictable. What works on the Tokyo stock market this afternoon may blow up in your face on the currency markets tomorrow. There are no absolutes. You have to judge each situation as you find it, and you just have to strive to be as objective and as rational as you can be all the time.

That said, conventional wisdom shouldn't be completely ignored. Having the discipline to cut a loss is vital. It can be the one element that separates a successful trader from his poorer cousins. Most of us can make money from time to time, the challenge is holding on to it and not giving it back without a fight. And above all, steps need to be taken to avoid heavy losses on individual trades.

Sometimes it's very difficult to face the fact that a position has not worked out and that it's time to pick up the phone and cauterise the wound. There's a fear that the moment you hang up, the market will turn. I know, because I've experienced that fear. And guess what? Sometimes, as soon as you've finished the call, the market *will* turn, and you will suffer the twin tortures of both losing money and knowing that you needn't have done so had you only waited five minutes more. The markets are like that. They make fools of us all from time to time.

But for every exasperating instance where the market turns, there will plenty of other instances when prices just keep running away from you. You always need to allow a position enough leeway to work, but once it goes sour, close it out fast. You can always get back into the same market later if you feel you must.

The proper use of stop-losses and controlled risk bets takes some of the anguish out of the decision-making process, and that's one of the reasons why you should always use such devices. It's also a good policy to decide how much pain you are prepared to take right at the start, when such considerations seem more remote than they might do when the margin calls are coming.

Stop-losses and controlled risk bets are always the last line of defence. Never feel that you have to run a trade right down to the wire. If a trade is going to fail, that fact will often become apparent quite quickly. A willingness to take small losses can save a lot of pain in the long run.

Knowing when to take a profit seems a less fraught kind of an issue, yet pressing home your advantage when things go right is just as important as protecting yourself when things go wrong.

Perhaps the most sensible advice is to run your profits but not to be stupid about it.

A few years back, I interviewed Jonathan Sparke, who at the time was MD of City Index. He expressed the view that spread bettors generally were a little bit too quick to take profits, often closing out and going off to celebrate if they were in front by the end of the week.

The idea that you never go broke taking a profit is a bit of a fallacy. It's no good frantically grabbing small gains every time they present themselves, and getting smashed for heavy losses every other time. If a position really starts to move in your favour, take advantage and let it run.

It is important, though, to safeguard positions once they move firmly in the right direction. Certainly anyone who ever lets a really good profit run down to nothing should frame the contract notes as a personal reminder never to let the same thing happen again.

The best way to lock-in a profit is to keep ratcheting up the stop-loss limit as the profits accumulate.

Section Four

Trading strategies

6 How to cut dealing costs

Spread betting is closely modelled on futures and options trading. That's its appeal – it provides an accessible, tax-efficient way for private investors to get involved in these specialist markets. But spread betting and direct futures and options trading are not quite the same thing. There are some important differences.

Perhaps the most important practical difference between spreads and futures is that spread betting normally puts the trader on the wrong end of wider margins.

An investor buying or selling an actual FTSE futures contract, for instance, might have to overcome a market spread and broker's commission on the deal equivalent to about five or six points. The same spread trade, depending on the contract month, the stake and the time of day, could cost up to three times more.

To be fair, this does not quite paint an accurate picture. The seemingly more expensive spread bet happens to include all costs, including any potential tax liability. The price is extremely transparent. The real costs of a futures deal could be every bit as steep, or even steeper, once capital gains tax liabilities have been allowed for. Even so, it's a fact that spreads bets are not cheap.

Now, on one level it's not worth getting too fixated on the costs of a deal. A great trade is still a great trade whether it costs you an extra couple of points more or not. And a bad trade won't be salvaged by fractionally lower dealing expenses. However, exceptionally good and bad trades tend to balance out. Over time, even the most successful traders probably generate profits of less than ten per cent on turnover, and in that context the transaction costs become a highly significant factor.

This is not to say that you should favour futures over spreads. Spreads still have that tax advantage and the staking levels are more in line with what most people can afford. But it does mean that a sensible approach involves taking steps to keep the dealing costs down to a realistic minimum.

Narrowing the spread

There are several steps that can be taken to minimise the spread you have to pay on a deal.

Firstly, recognise the fact that the bookmakers' margins are not fixed. There are wider spreads on certain types of bets than others. Unless there is a compelling reason to do otherwise, you should always structure your trades in such a way as to take advantage of the lowest spreads available.

In practical terms, for one thing this means doing something as basic as always trading during market hours. If you choose to deal late in the evening, expect to pay about 20 per cent more for the privilege.

Also, favour leading markets over more obscure ones. In percentage terms, the spreads on the minor markets are always higher than in mainstream areas, where there's more liquidity. This is because the spread firms hedge much of their exposure. It costs them more to deal in the minor markets and they pass this on. The result is that, to put it in simple terms, you have to be more right to make money betting on the Dax than the FTSE.

By all means if you have a strong view about the Australian dollar, go ahead and trade, but appreciate that the hurdles to be overcome are that much higher. So always be hyper-selective when considering positions outside the mainstream market sectors.

128 . Market Speculating

As mentioned previously, money management is one of the cornerstones of success. It's vital to maintain a bank and to risk only a portion of it on any one trade.

However, the spread firms find it cheaper to handle one large transaction than a dozen smaller ones, so preferential terms are always offered to higher-staking clients, as is the case throughout the financial markets. So without compromising your staking policy, bear in mind that higher-unit stakes are usually more cost-effective.

Just to hammer home the point, though, sensible staking features much higher up the list of trading priorities than trying to slice a couple of points here and there off the spread. If common sense and available funds dictate that you have to deal at minimum stakes for the time being, then so be it. Eventually, if you trade sensibly, make some money and build up your bank, at that point you can start to take advantage of those economies of scale.

The choice of contract month also has a bearing on the size of the spread. The longer a contract has to run to expiry, the more expensive it is to trade. Given that the overwhelming majority of spread bets are closed within a couple of weeks of opening, it makes absolutely no sense whatsoever to pay a premium for the privilege of trading a distant month.

To take a specific case in point, IG Index quotes its own unique Millennium FTSE market. Given that FTSE futures don't extend that far, this bet is an ideal vehicle, perfectly suited for any private investor with deep pockets who wants to take a very long-term view of where the London stock market is headed. The standard spread on the Millennium FTSE is 20 points, which is excellent value for a 12-month trade. It is, however, appalling value for a 12-day trade, which could cost as little as eight points. So unless you have a good reason to do otherwise, always trade the nearest contract month available.

There is one further important reason to focus on short-term contracts. In some cases, if you allow a bet to run to expiry, then no spread is charged on the close. This effectively halves the dealing costs associated with the trade. Taken by itself, this is not enough to make you run a position that you would otherwise choose to close, but it's an often neglected consideration worth taking into account if a contract is getting near to expiration. The rules in this area vary from firm to firm and from market to market, so consult a dealer if you are in any doubt. It's certainly the case at the moment that IG does not charge a closing spread on FTSE and Wall Street bets that are still open at expiration.

Finally, be a good consumer and shop around. The spreads firms all use the same data to frame their prices, taking up-to-the-minute quotes from Reuters and so on, so their prices will always be identical to within a few points

The dealers, though, do enjoy some latitude. Business ebbs and flows, and if one firm has seen more buyers than sellers, for instance, they might edge their prices upwards slightly in an attempt to balance things out, encouraging sellers and discouraging further buyers. If you have more than one account, it's always worth making an extra call just to ensure that you are dealing on the best terms possible. As always, though, remember that the different firms have different rules and you need to be certain when comparing prices from separate sources that the comparisons are valid.

Dealing frequency

Whilst minimising the size of the spread on each individual bet is important, it's only half the story so far as total dealing costs are concerned. The frequency of trading is even more critical.

Think of it like this: an investor opening and closing a £10 bet on the FTSE once a week for a year, paying the minimum eight-point spread each time, would run up total annual dealing costs of £4,160. In other words, he or she would need a 416 point move on the FTSE, correctly called, just to cover the spread.

Now imagine, for instance, if instead of trading the FTSE for £10 a week at an eight-point spread, the same investor were to trade for just £2 a week but with an 18-point spread. Over the course of the year, he or she would need to correctly call a market move of – wait for it – 936 points just to break even. That, frankly, is near impossible.

Market Speculating

For investors speculating directly with futures and options, which have slightly lower dealing costs, over-trading is folly. But for anyone using spreads, because of the higher costs involved, over-trading is just about the ultimate sin.

If you trade too frequently, you will lose money. It may not happen over a week or a month, but in the end the percentages are just too great to be beaten. Like a mathematical black hole, they will suck in and crush any investor daft enough to try to slip by.

The implications are pretty obvious. Spread betting has to be used not just with judgement but also with considerable restraint. The times you don't bet become every bit as important as the times you do.

Having the discipline to spot potential trades and to resist them is not easy. We live in a world where every day we are being bombarded with information and opinions from newspapers, from friends and colleagues, and from analysts and other commentators. Much of this might tempt you to chance your arm in the market. Indeed, the primary task of many analysts is less to analyse and more to stimulate turnover. The brokers, after all, are the super-dense material at the centre of that black hole sucking in unwary investors

So be selective. Wait. Trade not just when you think there's a good chance of a profit, but also when the downside risk is attractive. Screen out possibilities. Sometimes it may mean missing out deals that would have made money, possibly a lot of it. You have to resign yourself to such disappointments. Just keep reminding yourself that, if you over-trade, the numbers will beat you down in the end.

One of the best ways to cut down the frequency of trades is to reduce stakes and to start looking for slightly longer-term moves in the market.

Spread traders tend to have very short-term horizons and nothing is more conducive to over-trading.

One of the reasons why the typical spread bet has the life-span of a fruitfly, is, I suspect, because people tend to stake a little more than they should and as a result they get bounced out of positions too easily. With lower stakes, it becomes possible to set looser stop-losses, to tolerate bigger moves, and not to get whiplashed out of positions on the back of nothing more substantial than a day or two's fluctuations.

To illustrate the point, suppose you feel the FTSE will fall over the next three months. Rather than jobbing in and out and trying to ride the tides up and down each day, if you simply go short, but perhaps for a smaller stake than usual, and let the position run, your dealing costs collapse almost to nothing. A 12-point spread over three months is negligible, and if you get the market's direction right, you can make very significant gains – gains that are not eroded by heavy dealing charges.

Hopefully, the move by the industry towards lower minimum stakes will encourage more investors to start trading with smaller unit stakes and to take positions that reflect a slightly longer-term view of the market's direction.

... then again

Whilst researching this book I was very keen to get a sense of how the best spread traders operate. After all, you can theorise all day, but what really matters is what works in practice.

The spreads firms are always very discrete about client details, but IG did reveal to me how, in August 1998, one customer achieved what most of us can only dream about.

This unnamed client started with £10 bets on the FTSE. He called a few market moves accurately and gradually built up some profits. Using controlled risk bets, so that those profits were protected, he steadily increased his stakes and started betting on the US equity markets as well as the FTSE.

As August progressed, he continued to trade very actively and backed more winners than losers. In the space of about three weeks his stakes rose from the minimum, to £100, £200, even £300 a point.

Then, at the end of the month, he started selling Wall Street heavily - just before it plummeted over 500 points. One bet alone, and there were several, netted over £100,000.

In the space of four weeks trading, this guy dealt more than 150 times and made a clear profit, free of tax, free of expenses, free of everything, slightly in excess of £460,000.

In case you have never had a spread bet before and are about to trample the cat to death in a rush for the phone, let me point out that this is not a typical experience. What's more, anyone who trades that frequently has no right to make any money at all. Sometimes, though, that's how it works out.

The financial markets are crazy, unpredictable places. If you want to bet on them and make money, analysis and judgement are important. But a little bit of luck goes a long way too.

Section Four

Trading strategies

7 The ten golden rules

As far as making money on the financial markets is concerned, there are no magic solutions. What seems to work well today may not work at all tomorrow. Techniques that yield great results in one area might prove disastrous when applied to another. Each situation is utterly unique and the fine balance between risk and potential reward has to be judged each time entirely on its own merits.

Profitable trading cannot be reduced down to a series of simple steps, or indeed complex ones, that anyone might follow if only they had access to the blueprint. It's more elusive than that - far more elusive.

In the real world, success is the product of an unpredictable mix of experience, judgement, analysis, an indefinable 'feel' for the market, and sometimes even an element of luck. And in the case of each investor who finishes in front, the alchemy is probably slightly different.

And yet, even if the specifics vary from time to time and from market to market, there are still certain basic guidelines that do have an almost universal application.

These are the rules that most professionals follow most of the time.

Taken by themselves these will not turn a heavy loser into a feared speculator with the Midas touch. They may, however, help more seasoned traders to improve their returns. Perhaps more importantly, if followed consistently, these pointers will help steer newcomers away from some of spread betting's scarier pitfalls.

1 First things first...

Before trading, know the rules.

This may seem more than elementary, yet the fact is that many people do place spread bets without first being completely clear about how the relevant markets work.

Financial spread betting is quite complicated. A dealing handbook can extend to 70 pages or more without being totally comprehensive. What's more, rules can and do change from time to time. So it's only natural that not everyone is fully acquainted with every detail and contingency.

Novice spread bettors are by no means the only ones affected. Most experienced investors tend to concentrate their activities into one or two preferred areas, with the result that they may know all about equity futures, for instance, but rather less about currencies or equity options.

To trade without fully understanding the rules, and they way in which they are applied, is plainly asking for trouble. Mistakes can be made, and there is a particular risk that people may leave themselves vulnerable to far greater losses than they intended.

Before trading any market for the first time, carefully read the relevant sections in the dealing handbook and work through an example or two. If something is still unclear, ring a bookmaker of choice and speak to one of the dealers. The dealers themselves are used to explaining things and they much prefer to do so before a bet has been struck than hours later when things have started to go wrong. And don't worry about phoning at a busy time; someone can always ring back later when things are quieter.

It is impossible to succeed at spread betting without having a firm grasp of the basics, and nothing is more basic than knowing the rules of the game.

2 Consider the downside

Most spread traders are optimists, almost by definition. Whenever they trade they expect to make money; after all, why would anyone bet otherwise?

As a result investors, tend to focus primarily on the potential profits that might arise from a position.

We've all done it. Anyone who has ever sold Wall Street futures or the FTSE must have imagined, at least for a moment, precisely what it would mean if the market went into that long-awaited freefall at just the right moment.

However, the harsh reality – and one that no-one should ever forget - is that most spread bets lose money. Even the most profitable traders may back as many losers as winners and succeed only because they keep the losses under tight control.

In a sense, when weighing up a possible trade, the most important aspect of it is not what might be won, but what might be lost. Investors need to rein in their natural optimism and force themselves to pay at least as much attention to the downside as the up.

Before opening a new position, always ask yourself what can go wrong. And always give honest answers.

Above all, special care must be taken before entering into any deal that holds out the promise of a small but fairly safe profit, in return for assuming a very high degree of risk, as when selling options. It's no good making a few small gains only to give it all back and then some when things go badly wrong.

It's said that fear and greed are the two human emotions that drive all financial markets. Most spread traders would benefit if every time they dealt they felt a little less greed and quite a bit more fear.

3 Think for yourself

In the financial markets nearly all the advantages lie with the institutions. They have the financial muscle that lets them deal on better terms than private investors; they employ the best brains money can buy; and they have discrete access to all kinds of useful market intelligence.

Private investors, though, do have the upper hand in at least two rather more modest respects. Firstly, the ordinary investor never has to trade. If nothing appeals, we can sit back and wait patiently until something does. The professionals in the City, with those big salaries to justify, do not have the freedom to take a day off because everything in the market looks about right.

The other advantage private investors enjoy is that they are playing with their own money. They don't have to answer to anyone else and they have absolute unaccountable freedom to trade any way they see fit.

Professionals cannot do this. They have to think benchmarks and targets, and they have to keep looking over their shoulders to see what the other guy is up to.

It's not in a fund manager's interests, for instance, to defy conventional wisdom, at least not to any meaningful extent. It's better to be wrong in numbers, safe in the anonymity that implies, than to be wrong in splendid isolation, in which case bonuses and even careers could be on the line. When people talk about crowd psychology in the City, they do so with good reason.

Admittedly the freedom to do so is not much of an advantage, but spread traders can and should think for themselves. They should constantly question the orthodoxy of the day. Markets do get things wrong and that creates incredible opportunities for maverick private investors with the courage to back their convictions. Remember, the way to make money in the markets is to be right. But the way to make really big money is to be right when everyone else is wrong.

This is not to say that small investors should gratuitously run against the herd. That's a great way to get trampled to death. It's merely an acknowledgement that people can make more money if they make up their own minds and think for themselves.

4 Use appropriate risk management techniques

Given that most spread bets end up in negative territory, it's vital to deal with losing positions correctly every time.

Spread betting provides a range of techniques that can be used to cap losses if things go wrong, such as stop-losses and controlled risk bets. Most investors should use one or other of these techniques every time they trade. Novice investors, or those with limited spread betting experience, should take particular care.

When using controlled risk bets, it is a good idea to pitch stops around key technical support and resistance levels, where the market is most likely to move in a sharply negative direction.

Never lose sight of the fact, though, that these methods represent nothing more than the last line of defence in the overall risk control process. If bets routinely go wrong right up to the limit, it becomes almost impossible to make money. So aim to identify and cut losses as early as possible.

If a deal is going to work out, it often becomes apparent quite quickly. If not, don't hesitate to close out. Every investor should be comfortable taking small losses. So long as people keep enough of their capital intact, there is always the option of re-opening a similar position when market conditions seem more favourable.

5 Think short-term

In a world where we are all constantly urged to look to the future, it seems almost paradoxical to concentrate purely on the next few hours or days. Yet spread betting is not direct equity investment where weekly and monthly fluctuations can be ignored. The typical spread bet lasts barely a week. There are good reasons why investors should try to stretch that period, but the fact remains that most investors use spread betting for very short-term speculation, and that demands thinking in an appropriately short-term way.

For one thing, timing becomes vital. There are no points awarded for moral victories, or for being vindicated six weeks after being blown out of a position. It is not enough to be right. You need to be right, right now.

The essence of short-term trading is to react to market moves, not to try to anticipate them.

Financial markets, for instance, have a propensity to overshoot. Identifying such excesses is one thing. Trying to predict exact turning points, to within maybe two or three days, is quite another. In fact, correctly calling a market top or bottom is more or less impossible, and when it happens it says far more about an investor's luck than about his or her judgement.

Most successful approaches to spread betting involve identifying trends that are already to some extent underway in the market and then running with them.

There is still scope for longer-term thinking, and even for a degree of contrarianism. But when the herd is charging off in the wrong direction, as it does from time to time, unless an investor has very deep pockets and can afford to suffer a lot of short-term pain, it's just too risky to bet against the stampede. The smarter option is to watch and wait, and to join in quickly when the market changes direction.

Technical analysis plays a big role in short-term trading. Investors should make it their business to learn more about such basic concepts as trendlines, moving averages, Fibonacci retracements and so on, as these can all shape the direction of a market in the short-term.

6 Minimise dealing costs and don't over-trade

The actual process of trading is costly.

The spreads that are paid every time a deal is done soon add up. Remember, a £10 bet opened and closed on the FTSE once a week for a year will, in effect, cost over £4,000. That means the trader needs a favourable 500-point move on the index just to break even.

Anyone who trades with that sort of frequency will find it desperately hard to show a profit over time.

The wider the spreads, the harder it is to make money. So it is important to ensure that spreads are as narrow as possible. This means trading mainstream markets in preference to more obscure ones.

Also, as most spread bets are closed in a matter of days, it nearly always makes sense to choose the nearest contract month available. It will have most liquidity and will be cheapest to trade.

In addition, it's generally more cost-effective to bet in larger amounts than small, though this fact alone should never persuade people to bet more than they otherwise would.

A good way to cut dealing costs is to try to take a slightly longer-term view and to increase the average length of time over which a position is kept open. This involves setting looser stop-losses and enough capital to ride out short-term fluctuations. For most people this is only possible if they reduce stakes. Fortunately this is now becoming an option.

It is hard to make money spread betting. Even successful traders only make a small percentage return on turnover, and cutting dealing costs is central to maximising that return.

7 Stake sensibly and maintain a bank

It is impossible to roll relentlessly on from one profitable trade to another. Losing money from time to time is an integral part of the trading experience.

Everyone who decides to spread bet must have enough capital to cope with these inevitable losses. Until investors can afford to lose, they cannot afford to trade. It's that simple.

The amount of capital needed depends very much on the kinds of markets that will be traded, the level of stakes, and the frequency with which bets will be struck.

Any investor should certainly have a large enough bank to cover five or six losses before starting to deal, and ideally much more than that.

Sensible staking usually means exercising caution. Most people would benefit if they staked just a little bit less than they felt they should.

The industry is moving towards accepting lower stakes and clients should take advantage of this.

The markets will still be there in six months, and next year, and the year after that. And so will the opportunities to deal. Forget about trying to get rich in an afternoon. The opposite is more likely to happen. Bet steadily, try to make money gradually, progressively build up more and more capital; and if it all works out, the longer-term profits will take care of themselves.

8 Specialise

In order to make money in the markets a trader needs a degree of expertise. It is impossible to be an expert on everything. Don't try to graze, meandering from one market to another, selling Japanese bonds today, European equities tomorrow, currencies the day after that, and so on.

The best way to build up worthwhile expertise is to select a few key markets and to specialise.

Narrowing the focus in this way makes it possible for an investor to develop a deeper knowledge and to cultivate a 'feel' for a particular market or group of markets.

Most people quite wisely stick to the markets that are easiest for private investors to track, such as the best-known equity indices, individual shares, UK interest rates and maybe some of the major currencies.

When following a market, it's a good exercise to try some imaginary trading, using the actual prices the spread firms quote. It's not the same as risking real money, but it does help to foster an awareness of the factors that drive markets. It's much cheaper to learn lessons this way than when hard cash is on the line.

9 Don't get carried away

It's not hard to make money on a spread bet. A market, after all, can only go up or down. A selection strategy based on nothing more scientific than the toss of a coin will still produce winners nearly 50 per cent of the time.

The fact that so many trades are profitable is part of the appeal of spread betting. But it also gives rise to a hidden danger.

When a trader hits a winning streak, as everyone does from time to time, it's easy to get carried away. The temptation is to start trading more often and to be less selective in the choice of bet. Very quickly staking levels can slide up way above sensible levels. The whole episode usually ends in one or two seriously bad trades and a horrible crunching mess.

Don't get carried away when things are going well. If something works, stick with it. Don't mess with the formula. Continue to be every bit as selective as before. Do not start trading more frequently, and keep staking levels under the same tight control.

10 Monitor performance

Everyone needs to keep detailed records of their trading performance and to review them from time to time.

These records should reflect more than the sum of debits and credits. It's a good idea, for instance, to note down why a particular trade was selected, what influenced the timing, why it was closed when it was closed, what was good about the deal, what was not so good, and what lessons might be learnt for the future.

Used properly, a comprehensive set of records can serve several valuable purposes.

For one thing, we are all creatures of habit, and that applies as much to spread betting as to anything else. By examining patterns of trading, it becomes possible to pick out the habits that help and those that don't.

When conducting this sort of analysis many investors find relevance in an economic theory known as the Pareto principle. This states that ten per cent of an activity accounts for around 90 per cent of the results.

The exact proportions will always vary, but typically a few trades will account for the bulk of profits, and another few trades will cover most of the losses. It's easier said than done, but finding ways to screen out even just a few of the worst trades can make all the difference in the long-run.

142 . Market Speculating

Section Five

Section Five

Investor protection and regulation

When you apply for an account with a spread firm one of the first things to become clear is that spread betting is comprehensively regulated. The applications forms, though straightforward, are long, extending to three or four pages. Then there's the fine print: a small library of tightly-drafted legal notices, disclaimers and caveats, all building up to the imaginatively-titled Risk Disclosure Notice, a document which successfully states the obvious in no fewer than ten easy-to-read sub-sections.

Sometimes it seems as if spread betting suffers from regulatory overkill. This is particularly true, incidentally, if you ever try your hand at sports spread betting; receiving a contract note through the post after a punt on Test Match runs was probably not what the parliamentary draftsmen had in mind when drawing up the relevant legislation.

However, even if things seem a little heavy-handed at times, the regulations exist to protect investors, and scrupulous enforcement is infinitely preferable to complacency or neglect.

Spread betting inhabits a peculiar twilight world. Though technically betting, the mechanisms involved are almost indistinguishable from those used in futures and options trading. And the amounts that can be won or lost are every bit as great. For that reason, the spread firms have been brought under the same regulatory umbrella as the more mainstream securities firms.

Section Five: Investor protection & regulation . 145

The regulatory framework

The principal piece of legislation governing the financial markets is the Financial Services Act, which was passed in 1986. Among other things, it made it a legal requirement for all investment businesses to be authorised.

The body charged with overseeing the financial services industry in this country is the Financial Services Authority (FSA), which has superseded the old Securities and Investments Board (SIB).

The FSA is in turn responsible for approving a number of Self-Regulatory Organisations, or SRO's. These organisations undertake the direct day-to-day job of authorisation, monitoring, and so on, within their own sections of the industry. The Government has made it clear, though, that it plans to streamline the system and eventually the SRO's will disappear and the FSA will take direct responsibility for the entire industry.

The SRO that regulates the spread firms is the Securities and Futures Authority, the logo of which will be familiar to anyone who has ever had a spread bet.

The SFA was set up in 1991, and it's a large organisation. It supervises approximately 1300 firms. Roughly half of these firms are British. The remainder are UK branches or subsidiaries of foreign businesses.

The SFA has five main responsibilities:

Firstly, it issues authorisation, without which no securities firm can legally do business. The process is extremely rigorous. Any company seeking authorisation must be judged 'fit and proper', as must those controlling the company. This means satisfying the SFA specifically in regard to integrity, competence, capability and financial soundness. Approval is not a rubber-stamping exercise. Typically it takes around three months. When William Hill – just about the most respected bookmaking name in the world – sought authorisation a number of years ago for a specialist sports spread betting operation, it took even longer than that.

Secondly, the SFA is responsible for monitoring authorised firms. It analyses financial statements and reports, and occasionally makes company visits to ensure correct procedures are being followed.

The third responsibility is enforcement. The SFA has the power to investigate firms and it can fine companies or penalise them in other ways if regulations are not complied with.

Fourthly, the SFA sets rules governing the services offered to customers. One rule, for example, prevents the spread firms from offering advice to clients. So don't bother asking your favourite dealer to recommend a bet. The SFA has to develop quite specific regulations that are broadly applicable across more than 1300 firms. Given that only four of those are involved in spread betting, it's scarcely surprising that not every detail is perfectly tailored to meet the needs of those of us who trade in this area.

Finally, the SFA has the important responsibility of monitoring the financial health of authorised firms. The SFA assesses risk-management policies and practice in each company. It also sets down strict guidelines dealing with the availability of capital, and so on. The spread firms are required to be extremely well capitalised. IG, for example, has a £5 million facility in place that it can call on should it ever be needed, and that's in addition to the ordinary day-to-day working capital employed in the business. All spread firms are safe, well-resourced businesses.

The investors compensation scheme

All private investors who open spread bets are protected by the Investors Compensation Scheme.

The scheme was brought into law by the '86 Act. It covers all firms authorised by the FSA, or any SRO, obviously including the spread firms.

The scheme is not government backed. It's funded by the industry, and all firms, including the spread firms, contribute a levy towards it.

The ICS is a rescue fund designed to bail-out private investors in the unlikely event of an authorised firm being unable to meet its liabilities.

The scheme only applies to private clients and it only covers debts relating to investment business. So tough luck if you're owed money for fixing the plumbing. Private clients are protected against losses up to a total of £48,000. The first £30,000 owed is paid in full, and then 90 per cent of the next £20,000.

The spread firms are extremely well-financed. Contrary to any preconceived ideas you may have about how bookmakers operate, the spread firms are also very conservatively managed. They survived the crash of '87 and it's hard to imagine them ever being unable to meet their liabilities. However, should a miracle happen, the Investors Compensation Scheme is there, and that £48,000 limit is high enough to cover practically all spread players.

Complaints

Given the volume of transactions and the amount of money at stake, the surprising thing about the level of disputes and complaints in spread betting is that it's so low.

Nevertheless, mistakes do arise from time to time. Dealers can misinterpret instructions or key-in the wrong details. Customers may not make themselves clear, or forget which way they traded.

When problems arise, they can usually be put right quickly. All calls to a dealer are taped and it's a simple matter to check back to see if an error has been made.

Beyond that, if a grievance arises, the SFA has a clear complaints procedure. The first step is always to speak to the firm concerned. In practice, the spread firms bend over backwards to be fair and will almost always give the customer the benefit of any reasonable doubt.

Failing that, the SFA runs an arbitration scheme. An application for arbitration cost £50, and though the SFA manages the process, the arbitrators themselves are completely independent. If the outcome is not satisfactory, there is a further appeals process.

The best way to deal with misunderstandings and other disputes is always to avoid them in the first place, and there is much that clients can do to short-circuit potential problems.

For a start, always make sure you understand the market you're trading. It may be hard to believe, but people do bet on markets they don't understand. If you're in any doubt, ask the dealer to explain things to you. They are always happy to do so. Also, be clear about the amount you stand to lose should things go wrong. Again, if in doubt, discuss staking levels with the dealer. And use appropriate risk control measures such as stop-loss orders and controlled risk bets.

When you phone, make your instructions clear and have the dealer call the bet back to you. Pay attention and make sure the details are correct. Going through this process properly – and it only takes few seconds – can prevent any number of problems emerging at a later stage.

After trading, it's a good idea to note down the details. Maybe it's just me, but it's infuriating a couple of hours later to start wondering whether you bought at 6067 or 6076. And always check statements. Mistakes can be rectified, but only if you spot them.

The legal status of spread bets

Until the middle of the eighteenth century, betting was regarded almost as a commercial activity, and bets were considered to carry as much legal weight as any other contract.

Unfortunately the courts gradually became clogged up handling betting disputes. In response, Parliament passed a law depriving bets of their contractual status. To this day, almost all bets, no matter how large they may be, are legally unenforceable. Bets are gentlemen's agreements with no legal substance whatsoever.

Spread bets are the only exception to this rule. Spread bets are contracts for differences, and section 63 of the '86 Act makes such contracts legally valid, but only under certain tightly-defined conditions. The contract has to be an investment and one of the parties has to enter into the deal by way of business.

Even this new law was not regarded initially as being cast-iron. It came into effect just before the 1987 stock market crash, when many people lost a lot of money, and until a test case was successfully brought there was a certain nervousness within the industry about how the courts would deal with spread bets.

The precedent has now been firmly established. Spread bets are fully enforceable in law. It rarely happens, but the bookmakers can sue their customers, and the customers can sue their bookmakers.

It is important, therefore, to spread bet responsibly. If you were to lose a million pounds backing horses on credit with Ladbrokes, as one City figure famously did several times over, in a sense, it's Ladbrokes that has the problem. But if you blow a million pounds to a spread firm, the problem is very much your own. You are liable for the full extent of any losses, so tread warily.

The regulatory trade-off

Financial regulation is a constant balancing act. On the one hand, the authorities have a duty to protect investors and to safeguard the financial system. On the other hand, they have to allow firms enough freedom to compete and carry out their business. It's always difficult to get that balance quite right.

To take a critical point of view, there's no denying that the current robust regulatory regime comes at a price. The absurdity of a risk disclosure notice is a fairly trivial observation. A more substantial point is that demanding capital requirements and other such restrictions impose costs on the spread firms, and these costs, inevitably, get passed on the consumer.

Moreover, heavy-handed regulation runs the risk of stifling or suppressing competition. Erecting artificial barriers around an industry may well screen out the unfit and the improper, but it may also deter reputable businesses, which might otherwise broaden customer choice and challenge the established firms in the industry.

When IG Index started trading on a very small scale back in May 1975, Stuart Wheeler, who founded and still runs the company, worked entirely from home. There's no denying that it would be somewhat harder for a spread firm to get off the ground in a similar way today.

Ultimately, though, the primary aim of regulation is to protect the investor, and the current system achieves this very effectively. The spread firms are obliged to conduct their businesses and advertise their services in a responsible way. Everyone who trades is made abundantly aware of the potential for loss. There is a strong, independent complaints procedure. Above all, if you are fortunate enough to be owed money by a spread firm, up to £50,000 it's almost as safe as having it in the bank.

Spread betting is an industry that needs to be regulated. It's possible to debate where the balance of that regulation should lie, but what is beyond doubt is that spread bettors are at least as well-protected as they need to be.

Appendices

Appendix One

Further reading

General

The Wall Street Journal Guide to Understanding Money & Investing *Kenneth M. Morris and Alan M. Siegel.* Simon & Schuster (1994)

Learn to Earn: A Beginner's Guide to the Basics of Investing and Business *Peter Lynch and John Rothchild.* Fireside (1996)

Technical Analysis Explained: The Successful Investor's Guide to Spotting Investment Trends and Turning Points *Martin J. Pring.* McGraw-Hill (1991)

The Visual Investor: How to Spot Market Trends *John J. Murphy & John L. Murphy.* John Wiley & Sons (1996)

The Disciplined Trader: Developing Winning Attitudes *Mark Douglas.* Prentice Hall Trade (1990)

Market Wizards: Interviews with Top Traders *Jack D. Schwager.* HarperBusiness (1993)

The Education of a Speculator *Victor Niederhoffer.* John Wiley & Sons (1998)

Introduction to Futures and Options Markets *John C. Hull.* Prentice Hall (1998)

Appendix One: Further reading

Keys to Investing in Options and Futures (2nd Edition) (Barron's Business Keys series) *Nicholas G. Apostolou.*
Barron's Educational series (1995)

The New Technical Trader: Boost Your Profit by Plugging into the Latest Indicators *Tushar S. Chande and Stanley Kroll.*
John Wiley & Sons (1994)

Futures

Trading for a Living: Psychology, Trading Tactics, Money Management *Dr Alexander Elder and Alexander Elder.*
John Wiley & Sons (1993)

Getting Started in Futures (3rd Edition) *Todd K. Lofton.*
John Wiley & Sons (1997)

All About Futures: From the Inside Out *Russell R. Wasendorf and Thomas A. McCafferty.* Probus Publishing Company (1992)

Technical Analysis of the Futures Markets: A Comprehensive Guide to Trading Methods and Applications
John J. Murphy. Prentice Hall Trade (1987)

The Elements of Successful Trading: Developing Your Comprehensive Strategy Through Psychology, Money Management, and Trading Methods
Robert Rotella. Prentice Hall Trade (1992)

The Futures Game: Who Wins? Who Loses? Why?
Richard J. Teweles and Frank J. Jones. McGraw-Hill (1989)

An Introduction to the Mathematics of Financial Derivatives
Salih N. Neftci. Academic Press (1996)

Trading 101: How to Trade Like a Pro *Sunny J. Harris.*
John Wiley & Sons (1996)

Options

Option Volatility and Pricing: Advanced Trading Strategies and Techniques *Sheldon Natenberg.* Probus Publishing Company (1994)

Getting Started in Options *Michael C. Thomsett.* John Wiley & Sons (1997)

Options as a Strategic Investment *Lawrence G. McMillan.* Prentice Hall Trade (1992)

The Options Course: High Profit & Low Stress Trading Methods *George A. Fontanills.* John Wiley & Sons (1998)

Black-Scholes and Beyond: Option Pricing Models *Neil A. Chriss.* Irwin Professional Publishing (1996)

The Option Advisor: Wealth-Building Techniques Using Equity & Index Options *Bernie Schaeffer.* John Wiley & Sons (1997)

Trading Index Options *James B. Bittman.* McGraw-Hill (1998)

Commodities

Futures 101: An Introduction to Commodity Trading *Richard E. Waldron.* Squantum Publishing Company (1997)

All About Commodities: From the Inside Out *Russell R. Wasendorf and Thomas A. McCafferty.* Probus Publishing Company (1992)

An Introduction to Commodity Futures and Options *Nick Battley.* McGraw-Hill (1997)

The Intelligent Speculator: A Unique Approach to Trading Commodities *Ralph J. Fessenden and John D. McDivitt.* Irwin Professional Publishing (1996)

The Four Cardinal Principles of Trading: How the World's Top Traders Identify Trends, Cut Losses, Maximize Profits, and Manage Risk *Bruce Babcock.* Irwin Professional Publishing (1996)

Forecasting Commodity Markets: Using Technical, Fundamental and Econometric Analysis *Julian Roche.*
Probus Publishing Company (1996)

Bonds

How the Bond Market Works *Robert Zipf.* Prentice Hall Trade (1997)

Getting Started in Bonds *Michael C. Thomsett.*
John Wiley & Sons (1991)

Damodaran on Valuation: Security Analysis for Investment and Corporate Finance *Aswarth Damodaran.*
John Wiley & Sons (1994)

All About Bonds: From the Inside Out. *Esme Faerber.*
Probus Publishing Company (1993)

Bond Markets, Analysis and Strategies *Frank J. Fabozzi.*
Prentice Hall (1995)

The Bond Market: Trading and Risk Management
Christina I. Ray. Irwin Professional Publishing (1992)

Appendix Two

Recommended Websites

The best source of general financial information in the UK is probably the *Financial Times's* website, **www.ft.com**. It provides a detailed overview of the markets and has a particularly good archive facility.

The *FT's* sister publication, *Investors Chronicle*, contains further information on individual companies. Its address is **www.investorschronicle.com**.

Bloomberg provides the City with much of its financial data, and the Bloomberg site, **www.bloomberg.com**, covers the global markets in some depth. This site updates the main US equity indices minute-by-minute and has a good equity chart service.

Two smaller US sites are worth a look: **www.stocksite.com** offers an independent commentary principally on US markets, and its lead columnist, Bill Fleckenstein, has been a notable bear of Wall Street for some time.

www.thestreet.com is an excellent site, which provides clear, accessible market reports that are updated frequently throughout the day. Unlike other sites, it also includes some coverage of futures and options, and there are regular features on technical analysis and other matters that may interest private investors. This site does charge a fee for access to some of their services, but there is a free trial period and it's certainly worth taking advantage of this.

The spread firms themselves operate some of the most sophisticated

Appendix Two: Recommended web sites . 157

sites around. IG is available at **www.igindex.co.uk**, and the competition can be found at **www.cityindex.co.uk**. Both sites display up-to-date prices and general dealing information. IG also offers an on-line dealing service, and the necessary software can be downloaded from the site.

All the major banks and brokerages have their own websites and many of these post analysis and research reports that private investors may find useful. Some may require registration, but try:

Natwest Global Financial Markets at **www.natwestgfm.com**
Barclays Capital at **www.barclayscapital.com**
HSBC Markets at **www.hsbcmarkets.com**

A good general research service is available from Lombard Street Research at **www.lombard-st.co.uk**. The site contains a mountain of quite detailed economic analysis, much of which is very relevant for spread traders.

A lengthy list of futures brokers from around the world can be found at **www.yahoo.com**, and it's worth browsing through some of these sites. The best Web presence by a UK broker is maintained by GNI, which has a site at **www.gni.co.uk**. Access to the site is free and it contains a good futures-orientated market report updated throughout the day, as well as occasional trading advice.

158 . Market Speculating

ODDS On

The alternative racing & sports monthly

stay
ahead
of the
field!

subscribe today!

Over the year you will receive around 700 pages of topical and illuminating copy to keep you well informed at all times. If you aim to make the game pay, it's a quality investment. And cheap at the price!

Along with detailed professional coverage of horse racing, the **Odds On** team are also experts in other sports and even in financial spread betting. Add the latest in the computer world and incisive, frequently controversial comment, and you have a unique package.

You can't afford to be without it!

To subscribe to **Odds On**, simply fill in the form below and not only save 10% but also receive a **Timeform Racecard** of your choice (worth £5.50)

You get 11 issues, including a bumper one for December/January.

Get your copy hot off the presses!

FOR ALL NEW SUBSCRIBERS!
FREE
TIMEFORM RACE CARD WORTH £5.50

credit card hotline
VISA MasterCard DELTA SWITCH

01691 679 111

To: **Subscription Dept, Rowton Press Ltd, PO Box 10, Oswestry, Shropshire SY11 1RB**

Please arrange a subscription to **Odds On** commencing with the _____ issue.

I enclose a cheque made payable to **Rowton Press Ltd** for **£23** *(£31 within Europe and £37 outside Europe to cover Air Mail postage)*,

or debit my Visa/Access card.

Expiry date: _____

Signature _____

Name _____

Address _____

_____

Code _____

ROWTON PRESS
The racing and sports publishers

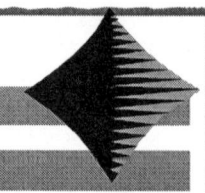

The Inside Track — The professional approach

Alan Potts is a full-time professional punter, author of *Against The Crowd* and a columnist in the monthly magazine *Odds On*. He is a regular speaker at club events, has been featured on LWT television, BBC Radio 5, The Sunday Times, Sporting Life and many other regional newspapers.

The Inside Track describes the methods Alan used to generate over £50,000 profit from his betting during 1997.

"If you entertain any pretensions at all to being a professional punter, or even adopt a professional approach to your weekend punting, you must read **The Inside Track**. Indeed if you only read one racing book this year, it has to be this one." **Malcolm Heyhoe, Racing Post Weekender** • "contains plenty of well-researched reasoning which will give even the most cynical reader plenty of food for thought. ... this office-bound pundit recommends acquiring a copy forthwith." **Mark Costello, Irish Field** • "Alan has developed a very individual method to winner-finding and explains many of his techniques in his excellent new book **The Inside Track**." **Lee Mckenzie, Raceform Update** • "... if you are serious about winning, become a better punter. Don't just think about it ... do it. Buy this book and give yourself a chance." **Luca Bercelli, Odds On Magazine** • "quite one of the most illuminating books on betting that you will come across ... an irresistible combination, packed with common-sense and written with a stoical approach that will strike a chord with punters" **Steve Simpson, The Gazette**   **Hardback, £18.00**

Spread Betting

Andrew Burke has worked for several bookmakers and in 1993 began the country's first column devoted to spread betting in *Odds On* magazine. In this book he offers a comprehensive view of spread betting, detailing all the basics and then going on to examine more complex areas such as value, risk and how to form markets.

This uniquely valuable and clearly written guide has plenty for novice and experienced players alike.
Foreword by Compton Hellyer, Chairman of Sporting Index

"Each chapter on football, racing and other sports is cram full of ideas, information, formulae for working out certain markets and sound advice" **Paul Kealy, Racing Post** • "the best and most informative guide I have read" **Ian Carnaby, Odds On**   **£8.95**

Betting for a Living

Nick Mordin. Nick Mordin is best known for his columns that appear monthly in *Odds On* magazine and weekly in the *Racing Post Weekender*. The systems he devises and tests are the result of intensive research and have won high praise from fellow racing journalists and generated an ever-growing mail-bag from fascinated readers.

During the winter of 1991/92, Nick applied his ideas at the racetrack, aiming to show that it was possible to earn a living wage from betting. In this book he tells how he succeeded in his goal, taking more than £1,000 a month from bookmakers, despite betting almost exclusively on week-ends and public holidays.

The book details the exact methods he used and explains the precise reasons behind every bet made. Reading it, Nick says, "won't turn you into a professional gambler, but will give you the knowledge you need to become one." First published late 1992. Now in its 9th REPRINT   **Hardback, £18.00**

Other top-selling titles include: • **Against the Crowd** by Alan Potts • **The Winning Look** by Nick Mordin • **Mordin on Time** by Nick Mordin • **100 Hints** by Mark Coton • **Coups & Cons** by Graham Sharpe

---

For credit card orders please call VISA **01691 679111**

or send cheque or PO to: **Rowton Press Ltd, PO Box 10, Oswestry, Shropshire SY11 1RB.**

Please add £1.50/ORDER for P&P within UK. For EUROPE please add £1.50/BOOK, OUTSIDE EUROPE add £1.90/BOOK

ORDER FORM *Please send me:*

____ **The Inside Track** by Alan Potts @ £18.00
____ **Spread Betting** by Andrew Burke @ £8.95
____ **Betting for a Living** by Nick Mordin @ £18.00
____ **Against The Crowd** by Alan Potts @ £8.95
____ **The Winning Look** by Nick Mordin @ £9.95
____ **Mordin on Time** by Nick Mordin @ £9.95
____ **100 Hints** by Mark Coton @ £11.95
____ **Coups & Cons** by Graham Sharpe @ £4.95

I enclose a cheque/PO for £_____ or please debit my VISA card

Expiry date _____

Signature _____

NAME _____

ADDRESS _____

Code _____   MS